CHINESE COOKING FOR TWO

BY
NANCY CHIH MA

TRANSLATED BY
MITSUKI KOVACS

GRACE ZIA CHU
CONSULTANT

BARRON'S

First U.S. edition 1980 by Barron's Educational Series, Inc.

Original Japanese edition published and © Copyright 1972
by Kodansha Ltd., Tokyo

All inquiries should be addressed to:
Barron's Educational Series, Inc.
250 Wireless Boulevard
Hauppauge, NY 11788

Library of Congress Catalog Card Number 79-12919

International Standard Book Number
    0-8120-5267-6 (cloth edition)
    0-8120-4770-2 (paper edition)

Library of Congress Cataloging-in-Publication Data

Ma, Po-ch'ang Ch'ih.
    Chinese cooking for two.

    Includes index.
    1. Cookery, Chinese.   I. Title
TX724.5.C5M17   641.5'61   79-12919
ISBN 0-8120-5267-6
ISBN 0-8120-4770-2 (pbk)

PRINTED IN HONG KONG

1234   4900   987654321

Contents

Introduction

CHINESE COOKING FOR TWO is a cookbook for *anyone* interested in Chinese cooking. The author knows the needs of the reader and keeps them in mind throughout the book. The directions are clear and the measurements are laid down just as clearly. For each recipe there is a beautiful photograph of the completed dish, along with step-by-step pictures for the novice to follow.

The dishes chosen cover the full range of meats, poultry and vegetables. They follow the Chinese banquet order of cold combination platters (appetizers), main courses, vegetables, starchy dishes, soups, pot dishes, and desserts to round up the meal. Basic techniques of cooking and cutting are carefully explained. A glossary of ingredients is included in a special section at the end of the book.

Such a book, with its easy to obtain ingredients and simple directions, will help anyone to prepare an interesting and nutritious Chinese meal.

— MADAME GRACE CHU

CHINESE COOKING FOR TWO

1. Remove all the mud and clean under cold running water. Dry with paper towel.

2. Crack the egg shell lightly with back of wooden spoon, then clean the egg thoroughly. Shell carefully as egg whites are very soft and delicate.

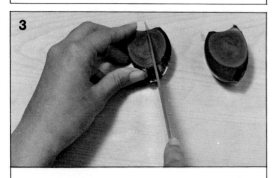

3. When the egg is cleaned, cut it lengthwise into 4 to 6 wedges and put on a plate. Sprinkle with soy sauce and the juice of fresh ginger.

Hors d'Oeuvre

Thousand-Year-Old Eggs

4 THOUSAND-YEAR-OLD EGGS
½ TEASPOON SOY SAUCE
½ TEASPOON FRESH GINGER JUICE

Jellyfish Salad

2 OUNCES JELLYFISH
1 TABLESPOON SESAME SEED OIL
¼ TEASPOON SOY SAUCE
1 TABLESPOON SAKE OR DRY SHERRY
½ TEASPOON SUGAR

1. Shred jellyfish and soak for a few hours, changing water several times. Drain.

2. Put jellyfish in a bowl and pour warm water over. Hot water will make the jellyfish too curly. Drain and add sesame seed oil, soy sauce, wine and sugar. Leave for 10 minutes.

Soy Sauce Chicken Livers

6 OUNCES CHICKEN LIVERS
6 OUNCES CHICKEN GIZZARDS
¼ CUP CHOPPED SCALLIONS
2 SLICES FRESH GINGER, 1½ × 1 × ⅛"
1 WHOLE STAR ANISE (8 CLOVES)
1 TEASPOON SZECHUAN PEPPERCORNS
½ CUP SOY SAUCE
2 TABLESPOONS DRY SHERRY
1 TABLESPOON SUGAR

1. Wash chicken livers and gizzards and drain. Put them in a pot and add just enough water to cover. 2. Add scallions, ginger, star anise, Szechuan peppercorns, soy sauce, sherry, and sugar. Cook over moderate heat for 15 minutes.

3. Remove chicken livers but leave gizzards and continue cooking for 40 minutes or more, until tender. 4. Return livers to pot. Cool the mixture in liquid to room temperature. Cut livers and gizzards into ¼-inch slices. Serve cold.

Red-Cooked Mushrooms

8 DRIED CHINESE MUSHROOMS
1 TABLESPOON VEGETABLE OIL
½ TABLESPOON SUGAR
1 TABLESPOON SOY SAUCE
½ TABLESPOON SESAME SEED OIL

1. Soak mushrooms in 1 cup warm water for 20 minutes. Drain, reserving the water, and remove mushroom stems.

2. Heat the oil in a wok. Add mushrooms and stir-fry for 30 seconds. Add sugar, soy sauce, and reserved mushroom-soaking liquid. Cook for 10 minutes. Cut mushrooms in half and sprinkle with sesame seed oil.

Sweet Pickled Cucumber

1 CUCUMBER
1 TABLESPOON VEGETABLE OIL
½ TEASPOON SALT
1 TEASPOON SUGAR
1 TABLESPOON VINEGAR

1. Peel and seed cucumber.

2. Cut into 2-inch lengths and slice each piece lengthwise into 3 pieces.

3. Heat the oil and stir-fry cucumbers for a few minutes before the juice is given off. Add salt, sugar, and vinegar. Remove from the heat and cool. Arrange hors d'oeuvre on a platter along with sliced tomatoes and sliced abalone.

*Chinese
Fried
Chicken*

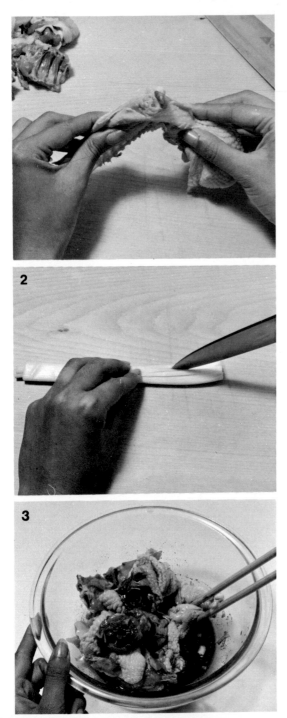

Meat and Poultry

Chinese Fried Chicken

COOKING TIME: 1 hour
CALORIES PER SERVING: 335
PROTEIN PER SERVING: 23.5 g

¼ CUP COARSE SALT
3 TABLESPOONS SZECHUAN
   PEPPERCORNS
1 SMALL CHICKEN
2 SCALLIONS
1 TABLESPOON SHERRY OR SAKE
1½ TABLESPOONS SOY SAUCE
1 TEASPOON FRESH GINGER JUICE
2 TABLESPOONS CORNSTARCH
VEGETABLE OIL FOR DEEP-FRYING

TO PREPARE ROASTED SALT AND
SZECHUAN PEPPERCORNS: Heat salt with
Szechuan peppercorns in a dry pan. Stir the
spices or shake the pan a few times,
roasting until the peppercorns are fragrant,
about 3 minutes. Cool, then crush in a
blender or with a rolling pin. Strain through a
fine sieve. This is used as a dip. You may
also use sweet and sour sauce as a dip.

1. Cut the chicken into serving pieces.

2. Chop the scallions.

3. Place the chicken in a mixing bowl. Combine chopped scallions, wine, soy sauce, and fresh ginger juice. Pour this mixture over the chicken and let stand about 30 minutes.

4. Add cornstarch to marinated chicken and mix thoroughly with chopsticks or fork. Do not dredge the chicken pieces individually, or the coating will get too thick.

5. In a wok heat the oil to 325°. Add the chicken pieces a few at a time. Cook, turning the pieces in the oil.

6. When chicken pieces are almost done, turn the heat to 400° and cook until the chicken turns golden brown and crisp. Drain and serve hot with roasted salt and Szechuan peppercorns as a dip.

Chicken with Cashew Nuts

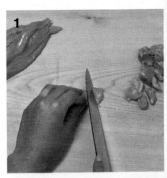

COOKING TIME: 20 minutes
CALORIES PER SERVING: 643
PROTEIN PER SERVING: 23.3 g

6 OUNCES CHICKEN BREASTS
½ EGG WHITE (ABOUT 1
   TABLESPOON)
2 TEASPOONS CORNSTARCH
1½ TEASPOONS SHERRY OR SAKE
½ TEASPOON SALT
1 SCALLION
VEGETABLE OIL FOR DEEP-FRYING
½ CUP CASHEW NUTS (YOU MAY
   SUBSTITUTE PEANUTS)
1 TABLESPOON SOY SAUCE
½ TEASPOON SUGAR
4 TABLESPOONS VEGETABLE OIL
1 SLICE FRESH GINGER 1½ × 1 × ⅛"

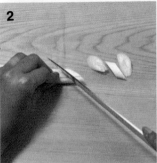

3

4

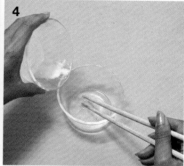

5

1. Cut the chicken into pieces 1 inch by ½ inch. Combine egg whites, 1 teaspoon cornstarch, ½ teaspoon sherry, and salt. Mix well. Let stand for 5 minutes.

2. Cut scallion in ½-inch lengths.

3. Heat the deep-frying oil in a wok over moderate heat. When it is hot, add the chicken. Deep-fry briefly. As soon as the color changes, remove the chicken with a strainer and drain on paper towel. Then deep-fry the cashew nuts in the same oil. Remove from oil as soon as their color changes slightly.

4. Combine the remaining teaspoon of sherry, the soy sauce, and the sugar in a small bowl. Combine remaining cornstarch and 1 tablespoon water in another bowl; set aside.

5. Heat 4 tablespoons of oil in wok. Add the scallions and ginger. Stir-fry for 1 minute, then add chicken. Add sauce mixture and mix well. Add cashew nuts.

6. Pour cornstarch mixture over the chicken. Stir until the sauce thickens. Remove from the heat and serve hot.

Chicken with Taro

COOKING TIME: 1 HOUR, 10 MINUTES
CALORIES PER SERVING: 518
PROTEIN PER SERVING: 31.5 g

7 OUNCES TARO
10 OUNCES CHICKEN PARTS, CUT INTO
   SERVING PIECES
1 SCALLION, CHOPPED
1 TEASPOON MINCED FRESH GINGER
2 TABLESPOONS SHERRY
4 TABLESPOONS SOY SAUCE
VEGETABLE OIL FOR DEEP-FRYING
3 TABLESPOONS VEGETABLE OIL
1 TABLESPOON SUGAR

1

1. Peel the taro and cut it into 1-inch cubes. Place the chicken pieces in a bowl. Add scallion, ginger, sherry, and soy sauce. Mix and let stand at room temperature for 30 minutes.

2. Heat deep-frying oil in a wok over high heat. When it is hot, add taro. Deep-fry until taro is slightly colored. Discard the oil or reserve for another use.

3. Heat 3 tablespoons vegetable oil in a wok. Stir-fry marinated chicken for 2 to 3 minutes, then add deep-fried taro. Mix gently and stir-fry for 1 minute.

4. Combine 4 tablespoons soy sauce, 1 tablespoon each sherry and sugar, and 1 cup water. Pour this mixture over the chicken and cover.

5. Turn the heat to medium low and cook for 30 to 40 minutes. Stir gently several times during cooking.

Chicken with Mushrooms

COOKING TIME: 20 MINUTES
CALORIES PER SERVING: 375
PROTEIN PER SERVING: 20.1 g

2 SCALLIONS
5 DRIED CHINESE MUSHROOMS
7 OUNCES CHICKEN
½ TEASPOON FRESH GINGER JUICE
1 TEASPOON CORNSTARCH
4 TABLESPOONS VEGETABLE OIL
2 TABLESPOONS SOY SAUCE
1 TEASPOON SUGAR

NOTE: In stir-frying it is very important that the oil in the wok or pan be always heated to the smoking point. Adding ingredients to the very hot oil ensures that they will cook quickly.

To get best results, cut all ingredients the same size. Prepare sauce in advance. While stir-frying, you should always watch the food and not be afraid to adjust the heat if it seems either too high or too low for the ingredients.

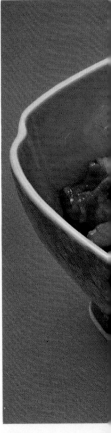

1. Cut the scallions into 1-inch lengths. Soak the mushrooms in warm water for 20 minutes; drain, remove the stems, and cut into 1-inch squares. Cut the chicken into 1-inch cubes and combine with the ginger juice and cornstarch.

2. Heat 2 tablespoons oil in a wok. Add chicken and stir-fry until chicken turns white, then remove.

3. Add 2 tablespoons oil to the same wok. Stir-fry scallions and mushrooms for 1 minute.

4. Add chicken and mix well.

5. Combine the soy sauce, sugar, and 2 tablespoons water. Pour this mixture over the chicken. Mix thoroughly.

White Cut Chicken

COOKING TIME: 45 minutes
CALORIES PER SERVING: 222
PROTEIN PER SERVING: 26.1 g

2 SCALLIONS
3-4 WHOLE STAR ANISE
1 TABLESPOON SZECHUAN
   PEPPERCORNS
2 WHOLE CHICKEN LEGS
½ TEASPOON SALT
1 TABLESPOON SHERRY
SESAME SEED OIL (OPTIONAL)

This is a delicious, simple dish that can be
served as an appetizer. You may steam the
chicken in a bowl instead of boiling in
water. The juice from the steamed chicken
or the boiling water makes a delicious
chicken broth for later use. Do not discard.

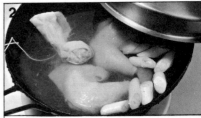

1. Cut the scallions into ½-inch
lengths. Wrap star anise and
Szechuan peppercorns in
cheese-cloth and tie with string.

2. Wash and dry the chicken pieces.
Place them in a wok, skin side up. Add
warm water to just cover the chicken.
Add sliced ginger and spices. Cover
the wok and bring the liquid to a boil.

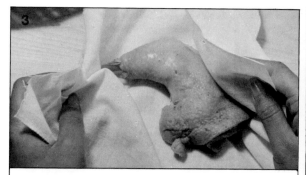

3. Turn the flame to medium and cook for 30 minutes. Remove the chicken and place immediately in ice cold water for 3 minutes. Drain and dry with paper towel.

4. Place chicken legs on a board and cut around the bone. Remove the meat and pull out the bone.

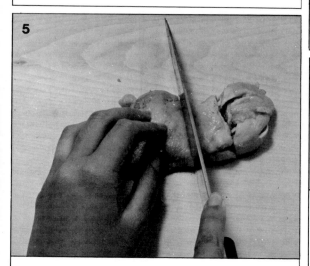

5. When chicken is totally cool, cut into bite-size pieces.

6. Mix salt with sherry and sprinkle over the chicken pieces. Brush the chicken with sesame seed oil or pour it over the top. Serve with sesame-flavored sauce.*

*TO PREPARE SESAME-FLAVORED SAUCE: Combine 1 tablespoon sesame seed oil, 2 tablespoons soy sauce, and ¼ teaspoon sugar. Serve in individual dishes.

CUTTING HINT: Wait until the meat cools to room temperature. Remove the string and cut into ¼-inch thick slices.

Chinese Roast Pork

COOKING TIME: 1 hour, 30 minutes (excluding
                    marinating time)
CALORIES PER SERVING: 950
PROTEIN PER SERVING: 28.4 g

14 OUNCES BONELESS PORK BUTT OR
   LOIN
2 SCALLIONS, COARSELY CHOPPED
4 SLICES FRESH GINGER, 1 × ⅛"
3 TABLESPOONS SOY SAUCE
1 TABLESPOON SHERRY
1 TABLESPOON SUGAR
½ TEASPOON SALT
VEGETABLE OIL FOR DEEP-FRYING

NOTE: Leftovers can be used as appetizers,
sandwiches, or in fried rice or noodles with Chinese
vegetables. Leftovers should be wrapped in plastic
and refrigerated.

1. With hands, cut pork into a cylinder 2 to
2¼ inches in diameter.

1

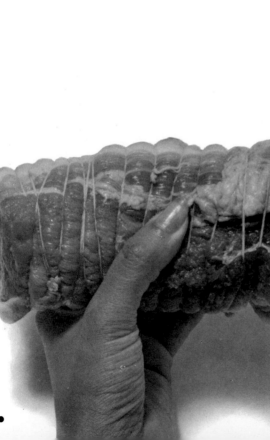

2. Tie tightly with a string, running around the roll. Tie strings securely at ends.

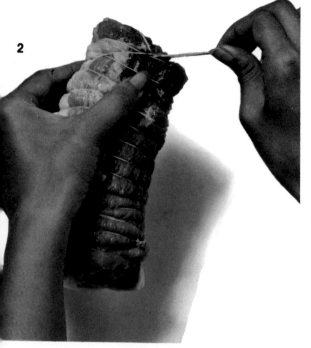

3. In a bowl combine the scallion, ginger, soy sauce, sherry, sugar, and salt. Marinate the pork in this mixture overnight or at least 4-5 hours, turning occasionally.

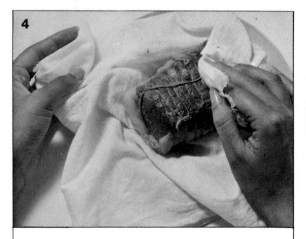

4. Place the meat in a pot with marinade and add enough water to just cover the pork. Cook over medium heat for 1 hour. Remove the wipe with paper towel.

5. Heat the oil over high heat. When hot, add pork and deep-fry, turning with chopsticks or wooden spoon until surface is golden brown and crispy. Remove and drain. When pork cools, remove strings and cut into ¼-inch thick slices. Serve with Chinese hot mustard.

Pork with Bean Paste

COOKING TIME: 15 minutes
CALORIES PER SERVING: 437
PROTEIN PER SERVING: 12 g

¼ POUND FRESH GREEN PEAS
¼ POUND LEAN PORK
1 SCALLION
3 TABLESPOONS VEGETABLE OIL
1 TEASPOON MINCED FRESH GINGER
1 TABLESPOON BEAN PASTE OR HAISEN
   SAUCE
2½ TEASPOONS SHERRY
½ TEASPOON SUGAR
1 TEASPOON SOY SAUCE
1 TEASPOON SESAME SEED OIL

1. Cook the green peas in boiling salted water for 1 minute. Drain well. Set aside. (Frozen peas can be substituted.)

2. Cut pork into ½-inch pieces. Cut scallion into ½-inch lengths. Heat oil in a wok. Add ginger and scallion and cook for 1 minute, then add the pork.

3. Stir-fry until the pork separates and the color has changed. Mix bean paste with 1½ teaspoons sherry and add to the pork. Mix and stir-fry for 1 minute.

4. Combine sugar, 1 teaspoon each sherry and soy sauce, and add to the pork. Mix thoroughly.

5. Add green peas then sesame seed oil. Stir and cook 2 more minutes. Remove from the heat.

Sweet and Sour Pork

COOKING TIME: 25 minutes
CALORIES PER SERVING: 827
PROTEIN PER SERVING: 21 g

SUGGESTIONS: Stir-fry the vegetables quickly over high heat so that they remain bright and crisp. Prepare all ingredients and seasonings in advance.

6 OUNCES BONELESS PORK BUTT OR LOIN
1 TABLESPOON + 2 TEASPOONS SHERRY
1 TABLESPOON + 2 TEASPOONS SOY SAUCE
VEGETABLE OIL FOR DEEP-FRYING
1 SMALL EGG
2 TABLESPOONS ALL-PURPOSE FLOUR
3 TABLESPOONS CORNSTARCH
½ CARROT
1 SMALL ONION
1 GREEN PEPPER
3 TABLESPOONS SUGAR
½ TEASPOON SALT
2 TABLESPOONS RICE VINEGAR
1½ TABLESPOONS TOMATO KETCHUP
3 TABLESPOONS VEGETABLE OIL
2 SLICES PINEAPPLE, CUT INTO CHUNKS

1. Cut the pork into 1-inch cubes and combine with 1 tablespoon each of sherry and soy sauce. Let stand for 10 minutes. Heat the deep-frying oil to 375°.

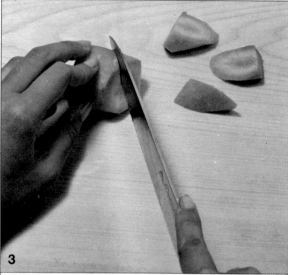

3. Cut the carrot obliquely and cook in boiling salted water until barely tender. Drain.

2. In a bowl mix egg, flour, 2 tablespoons cornstarch, and pork. Drop the pork cubes, one by one, into the hot oil and deep-fry for about 6 minutes, or until golden brown. Drain on paper towel.

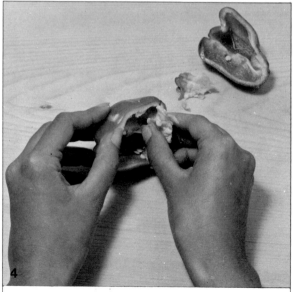

4. Cut the onion and the green pepper into 1-inch cubes.

5. Combine the sugar, 2 teaspoons each sherry and soy sauce, ½ teaspoon salt, rice vinegar, and tomato ketchup in a bowl. Dissolve 1 tablespoon cornstarch in ¼ cup water in another bowl.

6. Heat 3 tablespoons oil in a wok. Add onion, green pepper, and carrot. Stir-fry quickly for 2 minutes. Add the sherry mixture and stir. Pour the dissolved cornstarch over all and stir until sauce thickens and clears.

7. Add deep-fried pork and pineapple. Mix thoroughly and remove from heat.

Pork with Szechuan Preserved Pickles

COOKING TIME: 15 minutes
CALORIES PER SERVING: 350
PROTEIN PER SERVING: 8.1 g

¼ POUND LEAN PORK
3 TEASPOONS SOY SAUCE
1 TEASPOON SHERRY
1 SCALLION
½ TEASPOON CORNSTARCH
2 OUNCES SZECHUAN PRESERVED
  PICKLES*
2 OUNCES BAMBOO SHOOTS
3 TABLESPOONS VEGETABLE OIL
1 TABLESPOON SUGAR

NOTE: Szechuan preserved pickles are a
Szechuan specialty. They are preserved in salt and
hot chili peppers.

1. Cut the pork into matchstick-size pieces. Sprinkle with 1 teaspoon soy sauce and the sherry. Then coat with cornstarch. Cut the scallion into ½-inch lengths.

2. Cut the Szechuan preserved pickles and the bamboo shoots into same size shreds as pork.

3. Soak the pickles in cold water for 5 minutes and drain. Squeeze with hands to remove liquid.

4. Heat oil in a wok over high heat, add pork and scallion. Stir-fry until the pork separates, and its color turns light. Add bamboo shoots and Szechuan preserved pickles. Stir-fry for 2 minutes.

5. Add 2 teaspoons soy sauce and sugar. Stir-fry and mix thoroughly. Szechuan preserved pickles are salty even soaked, so do not use any salt.

Twice-Cooked Pork

COOKING TIME: 3 hours
CALORIES PER SERVING: 851
PROTEIN PER SERVING: 21.5 g

12 OUNCES FRESH PORK, WRAPPED IN FAT
2 SCALLIONS
2 SLICES FRESH GINGER 1½" IN DIAMETER
2 TABLESPOONS SHERRY
3 TABLESPOONS SOY SAUCE
3 TABLESPOONS VEGETABLE OIL
1 TEASPOON SUGAR
1 OR 2 WHOLE STAR ANISE
1 TEASPOON SZECHUAN PEPPERCORNS
½ TEASPOON SALT
5 OUNCES FRESH SPINACH
1 TEASPOON CORNSTARCH

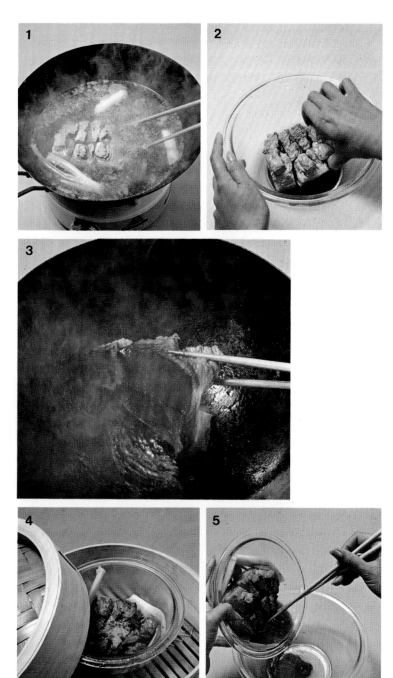

1. Score the pork ⅔-inch deep in 1½-inch squares. Cut scallions into 2-inch lengths. Put the pork in a wok or pot. Add enough water to cover the pork. Add the scallions, ginger, and 1 tablespoon of sherry. Bring to a boil, then simmer for 1 hour uncovered.

2. Remove the meat and place it fat-side down in a bowl with 1 tablespoon soy sauce. Let stand for 15 minutes.

3. Heat 1 tablespoon oil in a wok. Place pork, fat side down, in wok and cook until fat is browned.

4. Remove the pork from the wok and place in a mixing bowl. Combine 2 tablespoons soy sauce, 1 teaspoon sugar, and 1 tablespoon sherry. Pour this mixture over the pork and add star anise and Szechuan peppercorns. Add scallions and ginger which were used for boiling. Place mixing bowl in steamer and steam for 1 to 1½ hours over high heat, adding water from time to time if necessary.

5. When meat is cooked, remove it from the sauce, reserving sauce.

NOTE: Wet-steaming in Chinese cooking is very common. It is comparable to the oven in Western cooking because it is a self-basting method. Best results are obtained by steaming over high heat for the length of time called for in a particular recipe.

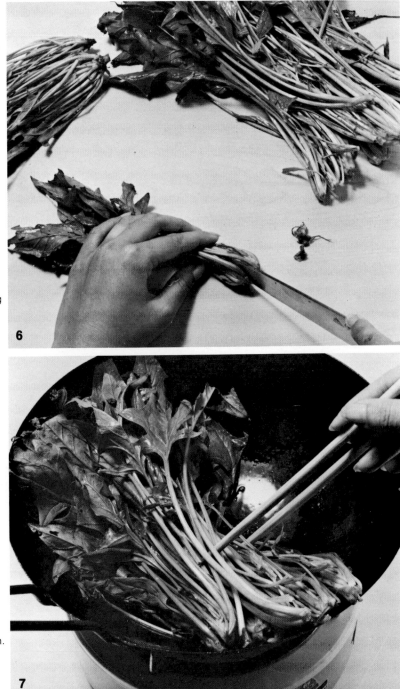

6. Wash the spinach under cold running water and drain well.

6

7. Heat 2 tablespoons oil in a wok. When it is very hot add salt and spinach. Stir-fry quickly. Mix thoroughly and remove.

7

8

8. Cut off the squares of meat from the bottom to which they are attached. Then turn over on a serving plate.

9

9. Arrange the spinach around the meat.

10

10. Boil the reserved sauce. Dissolve cornstarch in 2 teaspoons cold water and stir into the sauce. When sauce is thickened and clear, pour over the meat and serve.

Soy Sauce Beef with Eggplant

COOKING TIME: 55 minutes
CALORIES PER SERVING: 276
PROTEIN PER SERVING: 22 g

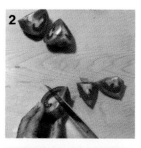

1 SMALL EGGPLANT
6 OUNCES FLANK OR SHOULDER STEAK
1 CLOVE GARLIC
1 TOMATO
½ ONION
1 GREEN PEPPER
3 TABLESPOONS VEGETABLE OIL
2 TABLESPOONS SOY SAUCE
½ TEASPOON SUGAR

1. Cut eggplant into diagonal pieces, and soak in cold water for 30 minutes (to keep it from turning brown), and drain. Slice the beef against the grain, and cut into 1-inch squares.

2. Peel the garlic and crush. Cut the tomato into 8 wedges, then cut in half crosswise.

3. Cut onion into 1-inch squares. Core and seed the green pepper and cut into 1-inch squares.

4. Heat oil in a wok over high heat. Add garlic, then beef and onion. Stir-fry until beef has slightly browned. Add eggplant.

5. Stir-fry until eggplant is softened. Add green pepper and tomato. Stir-fry and mix thoroughly. Add ½ cup water, soy sauce, and sugar. Mix well and bring to a boil. Cover, turn the heat to medium low, and cook for 15 minutes.

Szechuan Shredded Beef

COOKING TIME: 25 minutes
CALORIES PER SERVING: 442
PROTEIN PER SERVING: 21.9 g

6 OUNCES SIRLOIN OR FLANK STEAK
½ CARROT
1 STALK CELERY
1 DRIED HOT RED PEPPER
1 TEASPOON MINCED FRESH GINGER
1 CLOVE GARLIC
2 TEASPOONS + 2 TABLESPOONS SOY
   SAUCE
2 TEASPOONS SHERRY
5 TABLESPOONS VEGETABLE OIL
½ TEASPOON SUGAR

1. Slice the steak into ⅛-inch pieces, then cut into 2-inch-long strips. Cut carrot and celery into 2-inch-long strips. Remove seeds from the dried hot red pepper and crush into small pieces.

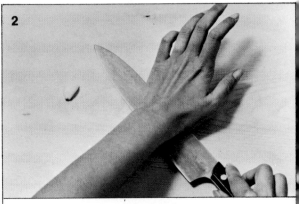

2. Crush the garlic clove with a knife. In a bowl, place the beef shreds and mix with 2 teaspoons each of soy sauce and sherry. Let stand for 10 minutes.

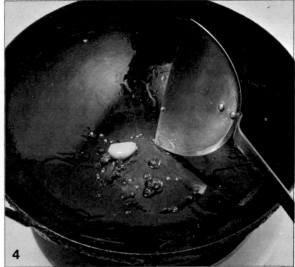

3. Heat 3 tablespoons oil in a wok. When it is very hot, add the carrot and celery. Stir-fry quickly for 2 minutes and remove to a plate.

4. In the same wok, heat 2 tablespoons oil, and add garlic and ginger. Cook until their color turns to light brown.

5. Add crushed peppers and beef. Stir-fry until beef shreds are separated and color changed, about 4-5 minutes.

6. When the meat is dry and no liquid remains, add cooked celery and carrot. Mix and stir-fry for 1 minute. Add ½ teaspoon sugar and 2 tablespoons soy sauce. Mix thoroughly and remove from the heat.

Stir-Fry Beef Shreds with Green Pepper

COOKING TIME: 20 minutes
CALORIES PER SERVING: 200
PROTEIN PER SERVING: 11.8 g

¼ POUND SIRLOIN OR FLANK STEAK
1 TEASPOON SOY SAUCE
½ TEASPOON CORNSTARCH
2 GREEN PEPPERS
⅓ CUP BAMBOO SHOOTS
3 TABLESPOONS VEGETABLE OIL
1 TEASPOON SALT
PEPPER

1. Slice the steak into ⅛-inch-thick pieces, then cut again into 2-inch-long, matchstick shreds. In a bowl, place the beef shreds and mix with the soy sauce and cornstarch. Let stand for 10 minutes.

2. Halve the green pepper and remove seeds; cut into fine shreds.

3. Cut the bamboo shoots into fine shreds.

4. Heat 2 tablespoons oil in a wok over high heat. Add beef shreds.

5. Stir-fry quickly until beef shreds are separated and color changed. Remove to a plate.

6. Heat 1 tablespoon oil in same wok and add ½ teaspoon salt, the green peppers, and bamboo shoots. Stir-fry for 2 minutes. Do not overcook green peppers. Salt keeps green peppers' color bright.

7. Add cooked beef shreds. Stir-fry and mix thoroughly. Add ½ teaspoon salt and pinch of pepper. Mix and remove from the heat.

Spicy Lamb with Sesame Seeds

COOKING TIME: 20 minutes
CALORIES PER SERVING: 474
PROTEIN PER SERVING: 9.7 g

6 OUNCES BONELESS LEAN LAMB
1 DRIED HOT RED PEPPER
2 SCALLIONS
1 CLOVE GARLIC
1 TEASPOON FRESH GINGER JUICE
1 WHITE OF SMALL EGG
3 TABLESPOONS CORNSTARCH
VEGETABLE OIL FOR DEEP-FRYING
1 TABLESPOON SOY SAUCE
1 TABLESPOON SUGAR
1 TABLESPOON SESAME SEED OIL
1 TABLESPOON VEGETABLE OIL
1 TABLESPOON WHITE SESAME SEEDS

1. Cut lamb into 1-inch cubes.

2. Remove seeds of dried hot red pepper and chop. Cut 1 scallion into ½-inch lengths and mince the other. Mince the garlic.

3. In a bowl combine the lamb cubes, minced scallion, hot red pepper, garlic, and ginger juice. Let stand for 10 minutes.

4. Stir egg white several times and add to the lamb. Add cornstarch and mix thoroughly.

5. In a wok, heat vegetable oil to 300° Deep-fry the lamb, a few pieces at a time, until outside is browned and crisp. Combine the soy sauce, sugar, and sesame seed oil.

6. Remove deep-frying oil from wok, and heat wok with remaining 1 tablespoon of oil. Add scallion and deep-fried lamb. Stir-fry quickly.

7. Add combined sauce and white sesame seeds. Mix and stir-fry until almost all liquid has evaporated.

THE RIGHT TEMPERATURE FOR DEEP-FRYING: To determine the temperature of your oil, drop a small amount of batter into the wok. If the batter drops to the bottom without surfacing, the temperature of the oil is lower than 140°. If the batter drops to the bottom and then rises to the surface, the oil temperature is 180°. If the batter explodes on the surface without ever sinking, the temperature is over 200°.

Fried Meatballs

COOKING TIME: 30 minutes
CALORIES PER SERVING: 536
PROTEIN PER SERVING: 11.7 g

6 OUNCES FINELY GROUND LEAN PORK
3 TABLESPOONS MINCED SCALLION
½ TABLESPOON FRESH GINGER JUICE
½ TEASPOON GRATED GARLIC
½ EGG, BEATEN
1 TEASPOON SESAME SEED OIL
2 TABLESPOONS CORNSTARCH
2 TABLESPOONS FLOUR
1 TABLESPOON SOY SAUCE
1 TABLESPOON SHERRY
¼ TEASPOON SALT
VEGETABLE OIL FOR DEEP-FRYING

1. Place ground meat in a mixing bowl. Add scallion, ginger juice, garlic, egg, sesame seed oil, cornstarch, flour, soy sauce, sherry, and salt. Mix very well, until the meat holds together. If not thoroughly mixed, air gets into meatballs and they will crack during deep-frying.

2. Scoop out a level tablespoon of meat mixture.

3. Using a teaspoon, scoop out meat from the tablespoon, then replace on tablespoon.

4. With a teaspoon, shape the meat into rounds. Continue making meatballs until all pork is used up.

5. Heat oil in a wok to 300°. Drop meatballs gently into hot oil, a few at a time. Rolling with chopsticks, deep-fry. Do not let the oil temperature get too high, otherwise the outside of the meatball will burn and the inside will be uncooked.

6. When meatballs are crisp and golden brown, remove from oil and drain. Serve hot.

1

Steamed Meatballs with Glutinous Rice

COOKING TIME: 40 minutes (excluding
  rice-soaking time)
CALORIES PER SERVING: 437
PROTEIN PER SERVING: 22.1 g

½ CUP GLUTINOUS RICE (SWEET RICE)
½ SMALL ONION
7 OUNCES GROUND BEEF
½ TEASPOON FRESH GINGER JUICE
½ EGG, BEATEN
½ TEASPOON SALT
1 TEASPOON SUGAR
2 TEASPOONS SOY SAUCE
1 TEASPOON CORNSTARCH
1 TEASPOON VEGETABLE OIL (TO BRUSH
  RACK OF STEAMER)
ORIENTAL MUSTARD FOR DIPPING

1. Wash rice and soak in cold water overnight. Slice onion very thin, then chop finely.

2. In a mixing bowl, place ground beef. Add ginger juice, egg, chopped onion, salt, sugar, soy sauce, and cornstarch. Mix until meat holds together. This makes 12 meatballs.

3. Drain the soaked rice, and dry completely. Spread it out on a plate.

4. Evenly roll 1 meatball at a time in the rice, then place the ball directly on a lightly oiled steamer rack. Leave a little space between each ball. Bring the water in the steamer to a boil. Set the steamer rack in place and steam meatballs over high heat for 25-30 minutes. Serve with Oriental mustard.

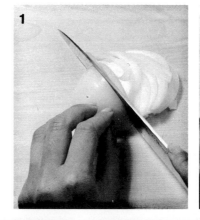

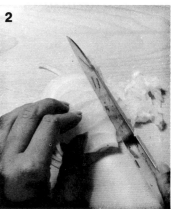

Fish in Paper

COOKING TIME 40 minutes
CALORIES PER SERVING 151
PROTEIN PER SERVING 17.4 g

5 OUNCES SOLE OR FLOUNDER FILLET
2 TEASPOONS SAKE OR SHERRY
½ TEASPOON SALT
1½ TABLESPOONS FINELY SHREDDED
  FRESH GINGER
8 SNOW PEA PODS
2 SCALLIONS
2 TABLESPOONS SESAME SEED OIL
8 SHEETS OF WAX PAPER (6" × 6")
VEGETABLE OIL FOR DEEP-FRYING

1. Cut the fish fillet into pieces 2½ inches by 1½ inches, to make 8 pieces. Marinate the fish in the wine and salt for 10 minutes.

2. Cut the scallions into 2-inch-long pieces, then finely shred lengthwise.

3. String the snow peas.

4. Place all the ingredients separately on a plate.

5. Grease the wax paper squares with a drop of sesame seed oil. Wrap ingredients.

6. Heat oil in a wok to 350°. Deep-fry packages a few at a time until packages turn golden brown.

7. Drain and serve hot.

TO WRAP INGREDIENTS:

1. Place wax paper sheets on table as indicated in picture 1/a. Fold bottom upward 1 inch below diagonal line, then fold the left and right wings toward each other. Fold the top over the bottom to overlap about 1 inch, then fold the overlap around the bottom. Open and pile 7 more wax papers underneath, then make 7 more folding lines.

2. Grease the wax paper with sesame seed oil using a brush.

3. On the middle of paper, arrange 1 snow pea pod, ⅛ of the scallion and ginger shreds. Place fish piece on top.

4. Fold bottom paper along the folding line.

5. Fold in the left and right wings.

6. Press the paper lightly and fold.

7. Tuck in corner overlap. Press to seal envelope.

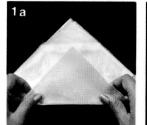

To eat, open the center of the fish wrapping with the chopsticks or with a knife and withdraw the contents.

Sweet and Sour Whole Fish

COOKING TIME: 1 hour, 30 minutes
CALORIES PER SERVING: 400
PROTEIN PER SERVING: 17.2 g

1 WHOLE CARP OR EQUIVALENT SEA
  BASS (1 POUND, 5 OUNCES
  APPROXIMATELY)
1 TABLESPOON SAKE OR SHERRY
4 TABLESPOONS SOY SAUCE
5 TABLESPOONS + 1 TEASPOON
  CORNSTARCH
VEGETABLE OIL FOR DEEP-FRYING
5 TABLESPOONS SUGAR
3 TABLESPOONS VINEGAR
1 TABLESPOON TOMATO KETCHUP
1 GREEN PEPPER
½ CUP BAMBOO SHOOTS
½ CARROT
3 TABLESPOONS VEGETABLE OIL

This dish is served as the final course of a full Chinese dinner.

1–5. Ask your fish dealer to scale and clean fish or do it yourself as shown in the photos. Leave the head and tail intact.

6. Wash and clean the fish, both inside and out, then dry with paper towels. Make 4 to 5 diagonal cuts, until knife touches bone on each side of fish. This allows interior of fish to deep-fry.

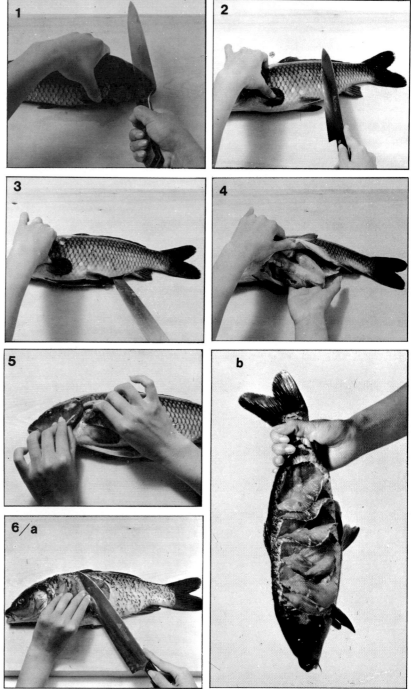

7

7. Sprinkle the fish with a mixture of wine and 3 tablespoons soy sauce. Rub 4 tablespoons cornstarch into the surface of the fish, inside and out.

8

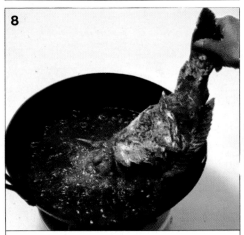

8. Heat oil in a wok to 350°. Lifting the fish by tail, slide it into the hot oil.

9

9. Reduce heat to medium. Deep-fry for 20 minutes. Ladle the hot oil over the part of the fish which is out of the oil.

10

10. Put a spatula underneath the fish and pierce the middle of the fish with chopsticks, and turn the fish over. Deep-fry until the fish looks crisp and golden color. Drain and transfer the fish to a serving plate. Keep warm.

11. Combine 1 tablespoon soy sauce, the sugar, vinegar, tomato ketchup, and a pinch of salt. Cut green pepper, bamboo shoots, and carrot into fine shreds. Heat 3 tablespoons oil in a wok, add carrot, bamboo shoots, and green pepper. Add combined sauce and bring to a boil. Combine 1⅓ tablespoons cornstarch with 1 cup water. Pour over the sauce and stir until it thickens and forms a clear glaze. Pour the hot sauce over the fish and serve hot.

Smoked Mackerel

COOKING TIME: 1 hour
CALORIES PER SERVING: 398
PROTEIN PER SERVING: 19.7 g

1 SMALL FRESH MACKEREL
2 SCALLIONS
2 TEASPOONS + 1 TABLESPOON SOY
  SAUCE
2 TABLESPOONS SHERRY
4 SLICES FRESH GINGER 1½ × 1 × ⅛"
VEGETABLE OIL FOR DEEP-FRYING
1 TABLESPOON SESAME SEED OIL

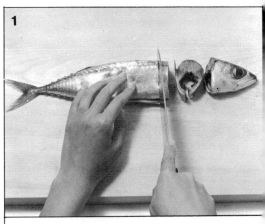

1. Rinse the fish, drain, and dry with paper towels. Remove the head and tail. Cut fish into 1-inch-wide pieces.

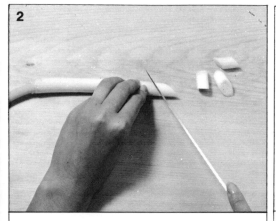

2. Cut scallions into ½-inch lengths.

3. Put the fish pieces in a mixing bowl and marinate with 2 teaspoons soy sauce, the sherry, half the scallion pieces, and 2 slices ginger. Mix well and let stand for at least 30 minutes. Turn the fish while marinating.

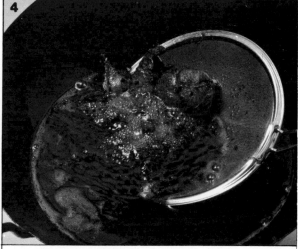

4. Heat oil in a wok over moderate heat. Deep-fry the fish a few pieces at a time (crowding will prevent the fish from becoming crisp) until they turn golden brown and crisp. Drain.

5. Remove oil from the wok and clean with paper towels. Into the clean wok, put remaining scallion pieces, sliced ginger, 1 tablespoon each sugar, soy sauce, sherry, and sesame seed oil. Cook over moderate heat until sugar dissolves in the sauce. Add fried fish pieces and cook for 5 minutes.

Puffed Shrimp

COOKING TIME: 20 minutes
CALORIES PER SERVING: 164
PROTEIN PER SERVING: 16.2 g

SUGGESTIONS: Use fresh, clean oil when deep-frying so that shrimp come out a white color. Beat egg white until stiff or shrimp will not puff when deep-fried.

10 RAW SHRIMP IN THE SHELL
½ TEASPOON FRESH GINGER JUICE
4½ TEASPOONS CORNSTARCH
½ TEASPOON SALT
1 SMALL EGG WHITE
VEGETABLE OIL FOR DEEP-FRYING
ROASTED SALT AND SZECHUAN
   PEPPERCORNS AS DIPS (SEE PAGE 10)

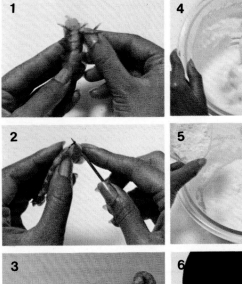

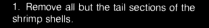

1. Remove all but the tail sections of the shrimp shells.

2. Remove the veins using toothpicks. Rinse, drain, and dry.

3. In a bowl combine ginger juice, 1½ teaspoons cornstarch, and the salt. Add the shrimp and blend well.

4. Start to heat the oil in a wok over medium heat. Meanwhile, place the egg white in a clean, dry mixing bowl and add a pinch of salt. Beat with wire whisk until the white becomes foamy.

5. As soon as the egg white becomes stiff, stir in 3 teaspoons cornstarch.

6. When the oil in the wok reaches 350°, hold the shrimp by the tail and dip them one at a time into the egg white batter, leaving the tail uncovered. Then place them in the hot oil and fry until the egg white is puffed. Serve with roasted salt and Szechuan peppercorns.

1. Shell and devein the shrimp. Wash, drain, and dry with paper towels. In a bowl, combine the shrimp with 2 teaspoons sherry, egg white, ginger juice, and ½ teaspoon cornstarch. Set aside.

2. Cook the fava beans in boiling, salted water. Drain and remove the skin.

Shrimp with Fava (or Lima) Beans

COOKING TIME: 40 minutes
CALORIES PER SERVING: 400
PROTEIN PER SERVING: 24.9 g

½ POUND SMALL SHRIMP
3 TEASPOONS SHERRY
½ EGG WHITE
2½ TEASPOONS CORNSTARCH
½ TEASPOON FRESH GINGER JUICE
1 CUP FAVA OR LIMA BEANS
3 TABLESPOONS VEGETABLE OIL
1 TEASPOON SUGAR
1 TEASPOON SALT

3. Heat oil in a wok; add marinated shrimp. Stir-fry quickly until shrimp turn pink.

4. Add fava beans. Mix and stir-fry for 1 minute.

5. Combine 1 cup water, 2 teaspoons cornstarch, 1 teaspoon each sherry and sugar, and 1 teaspoon salt. Add this to the shrimp. Mix and bring to a boil. Cook until sauce gets thick and clear.

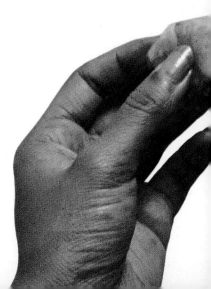

Shrimp Szechuan Style

COOKING TIME: 25 minutes
CALORIES PER SERVING: 409
PROTEIN PER SERVING: 11.6 g

5 LARGE RAW SHRIMP IN THE SHELL
1 CLOVE GARLIC
1 DRIED HOT RED PEPPER
2 SCALLIONS
1 TABLESPOON SHERRY
½ TEASPOON SALT
2 TEASPOONS SUGAR
1 TEASPOON CORNSTARCH
1 TABLESPOON TOMATO KETCHUP
3 TABLESPOONS VEGETABLE OIL
2 SLICES FRESH GINGER

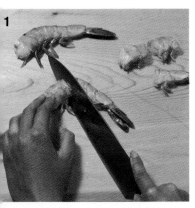

1

1. Cut the shrimp into 2 or 3 pieces, leaving the shell on.

2. Remove the veins using toothpicks.

3. Cut off the tails and the leglike pieces of shell.

4. Mince the garlic. Remove seeds from dried hot red pepper and crush. Cut scallions into 1-inch lengths. In a small bowl combine sherry, salt, sugar, tomato ketchup, and 5 tablespoons water. Dissolve the cornstarch with 1 tablespoon water.

5. Heat oil in a wok, add ginger slices, garlic, crushed dried hot red pepper, and scallion. Stir-fry for 1 minute then add shrimp.

6. When shrimp turn pink, add sauce. Mix and stir in dissolved cornstarch. Stir and mix until shrimp are well coated with thickened sauce.

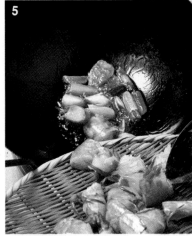

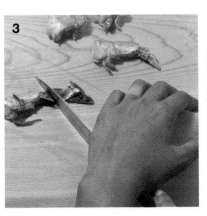

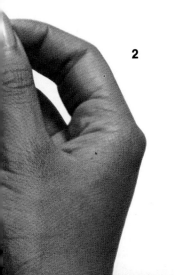

2

3

4

5

6

Stir-Fried Abalone
with Cucumber

COOKING TIME: 25 minutes
CALORIES PER SERVING: 214
PROTEIN PER SERVING: 20.8 g

1 SMALL CAN OF ABALONE
½ CUCUMBER
1 TABLESPOON SHERRY
½ TABLESPOON SOY SAUCE
1 TEASPOON SUGAR
1 TEASPOON SALT
1½ TABLESPOONS VEGETABLE OIL

NOTE: Fresh abalone is available in California;
canned or dried can be bought elsewhere. Canned
abalone is precooked and will turn rubbery if
cooked too long.

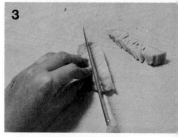

1

1. Remove external abalone membrane by hand.

2. Slice in half horizontally.

3. Make ¼-inch diagonal cut halfway down, then cut 1-inch-thick pieces against the diagonal cut.

4. Peel the cucumber and halve it lengthwise. Remove and discard seeds. Cut each half lengthwise once again. Then cut crosswise into 2-inch pieces. Make ⅛-inch-thick cuts halfway down each piece. Combine sherry, soy sauce, sugar and salt.

5. Heat oil in a wok, add cucumber, and stir-fry for 2 minutes.

6. Add abalone and stir-fry for another minute.

7. Pour sauce over the cucumber and abalone, do not overcook.

Red-Cooked Sea Bass

COOKING TIME: 40 minutes
CALORIES PER SERVING: 298
PROTEIN PER SERVING: 7.4 g

2 SMALL SEA BASS
1 TEASPOON SHERRY
5 TEASPOONS SOY SAUCE
2 SCALLIONS
2 SLICES + 1-INCH CUBE FRESH GINGER
4 TABLESPOONS VEGETABLE OIL
2 CLOVES CRUSHED GARLIC
1 TABLESPOON SUGAR
2 TEASPOONS VINEGAR

1. Remove the gills, stomach, and other organs from the fish but leave the head and tail on. Clean the fish with cold water and dry with paper towels.

2. Make ½-inch slash lengthwise on each side of fish.

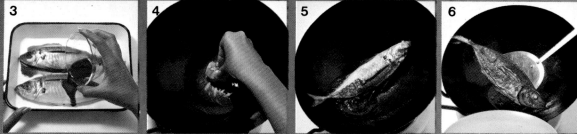

3. Place the fish in a baking dish. Combine the sherry with 2 teaspoons soy sauce and pour over the fish. Let stand for 10 minutes, turning a few times.

4. Cut scallions into 1½-inch-long pieces. Peel the ginger. Heat a wok over high heat. When it is very hot rub the inside with ginger cube.

5. Add 3 tablespoons oil to the wok. When it is hot, add fish and brown both sides.

6. When fish turns golden brown on both sides, remove from the wok gently with a spatula. Repeat with the other fish.

7. Discard the oil and wipe the wok with paper towels, then heat 1 tablespoon of oil in the wok. Add garlic, sliced ginger, and scallions. Cook briefly and add the fish. Combine sugar, remaining 3 teaspoons soy sauce, and vinegar. Pour over the fish. Cover and simmer for 20 minutes. Scoop fish carefully out of the wok. Pour the sauce over the fish and serve. If the liquid evaporates during cooking, add a little water.

Sweet and Sour Squid

COOKING TIME: 30 minutes
CALORIES PER SERVING: 276
PROTEIN PER SERVING: 17.6 g

½ POUND FRESH SQUID
1 CARROT
2 TEASPOONS SHERRY
2 TEASPOONS SOY SAUCE
½ TABLESPOON SUGAR
¼ TEASPOON SALT
1 TABLESPOON VINEGAR
2 TEASPOONS CORNSTARCH
3 TABLESPOONS VEGETABLE OIL
2 TABLESPOONS COOKED GREEN PEAS

1. Remove the tentacles and internal cartilage from squid.

2. Pull off tail fin and remove the head. Use only the bodies. Put the knife inside of body and open into 1 sheet.

3. Remove thin black skin by rubbing with salt. Wash under cold running water. Dry with paper towels. Cut the squid in half lengthwise, then make ¼-inch lengthwise slashes, but do not cut through the squid.

4. Cut the squid into crosswise, 1-inch pieces.

5. Cook squid in boiling water for 1 minute and drain. Do not overcook or squid will be rubbery.

6. Cut carrot into 2-inch pieces, then slice the pieces lengthwise, ¼-inch thick. Cook carrots in boiling salted water and drain. Combine sherry, soy sauce, sugar, salt, and vinegar in a bowl. Dissolve the cornstarch with ½ cup water in another bowl. Heat oil in a wok, add squid and stir-fry briefly. Then add half-cooked carrots. Mix and stir-fry for 1 minute.

7. Add sherry mixture. Bring to a boil and add dissolved cornstarch. Stir and cook until liquid thickens. Add green peas and mix thoroughly.

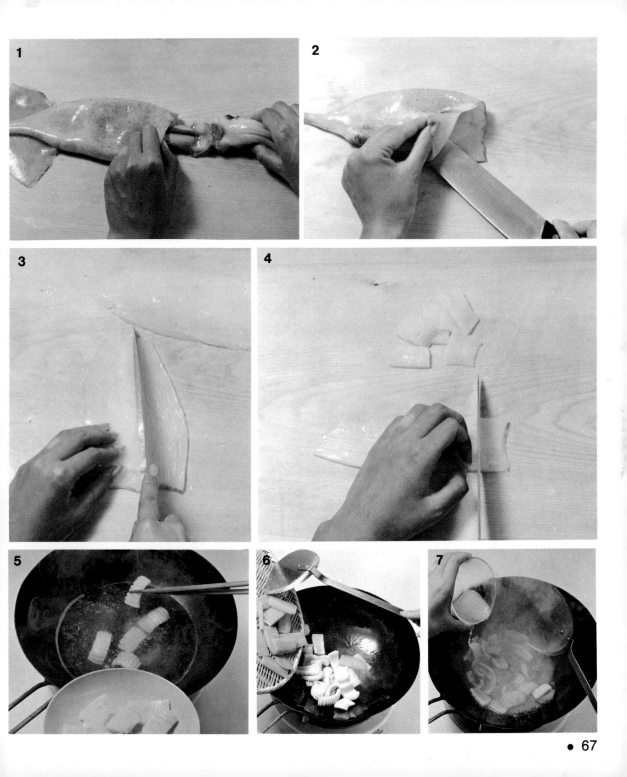

Vegetables

Chinese-Style Corn Fritters

COOKING TIME: 50 minutes
CALORIES PER SERVING: 376
PROTEIN PER SERVING: 12 g

2 EARS CORN
1 EGG
¼ CUP ALL-PURPOSE FLOUR
VEGETABLE OIL FOR DEEP-FRYING

1. Drop the ears of corn into boiling water. Cook for 10 minutes. Drain and let the corn cool. Cut off the kernels.

2. In a mixing bowl, combine egg, flour, and a pinch of salt. Add corn to this batter and mix well.

3. Heat oil in a wok to 160°. Drop a tablespoonful of corn mixture in the hot oil.

4. Cook until golden brown on one side, turn and cook until golden brown on the other. Drain on paper towels.

SUGGESTIONS: Do not raise oil temperature too high. If too hot, the outsides burn and the insides remain uncooked. Make batter first before frying. Well-drained canned corn can be substituted for fresh corn.

Happy Family

COOKING TIME: 50 minutes
CALORIES PER SERVING: 475
PROTEIN PER SERVING: 47.8 g

12 SMALL SHRIMP
1 TABLESPOON SHERRY
1 TEASPOON FRESH GINGER JUICE
3 TEASPOONS CORNSTARCH
2 SQUID (USE BODIES ONLY)
2 OUNCES GROUND PORK
1 TEASPOON CHOPPED SCALLION
2¼ TEASPOONS SOY SAUCE
VEGETABLE OIL FOR DEEP-FRYING
4 QUAIL EGGS
4 DRIED CHINESE MUSHROOMS
1 LEAF CHINESE CELERY CABBAGE
1 TABLESPOON GREEN PEAS
1 TEASPOON SUGAR
½ CUP CHICKEN BROTH
3 TABLESPOONS VEGETABLE OIL

*SUGGESTIONS: Be careful not to overcook.
Because every ingredient is precooked, cooking
time is short. Quail eggs come precooked, in cans.*

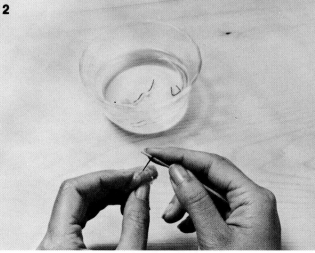

1. Shell and devein shrimp. Remove the tail.

2. Mix the shrimp with ½ teaspoon each
sherry, ginger juice, and cornstarch. Set
aside.

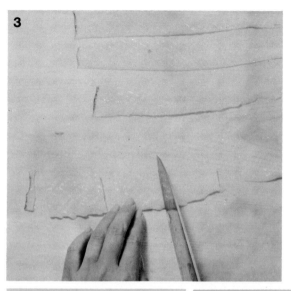

3. Remove tail and thin black skin from the squid. Split each squid into 1 sheet. Score each squid with diamond cuts, then slice into 1-by-2-inch pieces. Mix the squid with ½ teaspoon each sherry, ginger juice, and cornstarch. Set aside.

4. Mix the ground pork with chopped scallion, ¼ teaspoon soy sauce, ½ teaspoon sherry, dash of salt, and cornstarch. Mix thoroughly and make 2 meatballs. Deep-fry the meatballs in medium-hot oil. Drain when cooked.

5. Hard-boil the quail eggs in simmering water. Cool in cold water and remove shell.

6. Soak mushrooms in warm water for 20 minutes, then squeeze to remove excess water. Cut in half.

7. Wash Chinese celery cabbage leaf and drain. Cut into 1-inch squares. Cook briefly in boiling water. Cook green peas the same way. Drain.

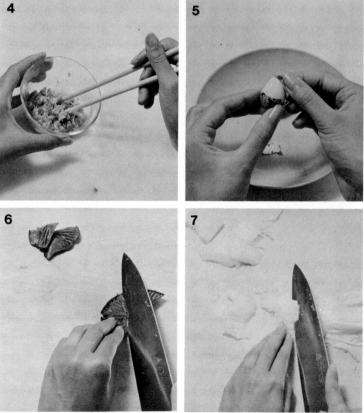

8. Combine 1 tablespoon sherry, 2 teaspoons soy sauce, the sugar, and the chicken broth. Heat the 3 tablespoons oil in a wok, add shrimp and squid. Stir-fry briefly until the fish change color.

9. Add meatballs, quail eggs, mushrooms, celery cabbage, and green peas. Mix and stir-fry briefly.

10. Add chicken broth mixture. Bring to boil and reduce heat to medium. Cook for 2 to 3 minutes.

11. Mix 2 teaspoons cornstarch with 1 tablespoon water and pour over the contents of wok. Mix thoroughly and cook until sauce thickens.

Stir-Fried Chinese Chives with Pork Shreds

COOKING TIME: 15 minutes
CALORIES PER SERVING: 308
PROTEIN PER SERVING: 8.2 g

4 OUNCES FRESH PORK
1 TEASPOON SHERRY
4 TEASPOONS SOY SAUCE
½ TEASPOON CORNSTARCH
3½ OUNCES CHINESE CHIVES (SPRING
  ONION)
2 TABLESPOONS VEGETABLE OIL

NOTE: Chinese chives are a green vegetable of the onion family. They are used for flavoring and sometimes as a vegetable. They are strong in taste. Chinese chives come fresh and are sold in bunches in Chinese grocery stores.

1. Slice the pork ⅛ inch thick, then cut again into 2-inch-long julienne strips to make about ½ cup. Marinate the pork shreds for 10 minutes in a mixture of the sherry, 1 teaspoon soy sauce, and the cornstarch.

2. Wash the Chinese chives and drain. Dry very well so they are not watery when stir-fried.

3. Cut off the tops of the Chinese chives, then cut into 2-inch lengths.

4. Heat oil in a wok. Add marinated pork and stir-fry briefly, until meat turns light. Add Chinese chives.

5. Mix and stir-fry until Chinese chives turn bright green. Add 3 teaspoons soy sauce and a pinch of salt. Mix thoroughly and remove from the heat.

Broccoli with Minced Ham

COOKING TIME: 25 minutes
CALORIES PER SERVING: 184
PROTEIN PER SERVING: 3.8 g

½ POUND BROCCOLI
2 TABLESPOONS VEGETABLE OIL
½ TEASPOON SALT
½ TEASPOON SUGAR
1½ CUPS CHICKEN BROTH
1 TABLESPOON CORNSTARCH
¼ CUP MINCED BOILED HAM

1. Wash broccoli in lightly salted water. Drain and cut off 2 inches from broccoli stems.

2. Peel the cut-off stems.

3. Then slice them lengthwise, ¼ inch thick.

4. Separate the florets with stems from the large stems.

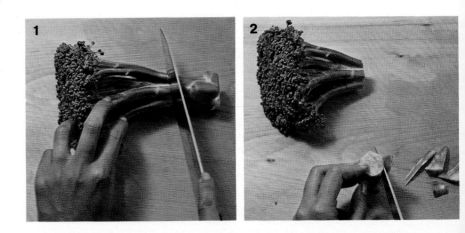

5. Cook broccoli and stems in boiling salted water for 2 minutes, then drain.

6. Heat oil in a wok, add broccoli and stems. Stir-fry for 1 minute. Add salt, sugar, and chicken broth. Mix and bring to boil.

7. Turn the heat to medium, and cook until broccoli is tender but not mushy. Mix cornstarch with 3 tablespoons water and pour over broccoli. Add chopped ham and mix gently.

Celery Cabbage Stuffed with Chicken

COOKING TIME: 50 minutes
CALORIES PER SERVING: 195
PROTEIN PER SERVING: 17.5 g

6 SMALL CHINESE CELERY CABBAGE
   LEAVES
4 TEASPOONS CORNSTARCH
7 OUNCES GROUND CHICKEN
¼ CUP MINCED HAM
2 TEASPOONS SHERRY
½ TEASPOON SALT
4 DRIED CHINESE MUSHROOMS
1 OUNCE CELLOPHANE NOODLES (½
   SMALL PACKAGE)
1 CUP CHICKEN BROTH
½ TEASPOON SUGAR
2 TEASPOONS SOY SAUCE

1. Cut off the bottom of the celery cabbage and remove the tough outer leaves; separate the leaves carefully without tearing. Cook celery cabbage leaves in enough boiling water to cover until leaves become tender and translucent. Drain and spread over paper towels. Dust inside of leaves lightly with 1 teaspoon cornstarch.

2. In a bowl, place the ground chicken, minced ham, sherry, salt, and 1½ teaspoons cornstarch. Mix until the meat holds together, then divide into 6 portions. Place the meat on bottom of cabbage leaf. Roll once, then fold the two parallel sides of leaf toward the center, then roll into a cylinder. Make 5 more.

3. Place 6 cabbage rolls on a dish one size smaller than steamer.

4. Cover and steam over high heat for 15 minutes. Soak mushrooms in warm water for 20 minutes and drain. Remove the mushroom stems, then cut each in half. Soak cellophane noodles in lukewarm water for 20 minutes. Drain and cut into 2-inch-long pieces. Mix 1½ teaspoons cornstarch with 2 tablespoons water.

5. When cabbage rolls are cooked, carefully cut each in half, then place in a wok or skillet in 1 layer. Add mushrooms. Combine chicken broth, sugar, and soy sauce and then pour over cabbage rolls. Cook over medium heat for 5 minutes, then add cellophane noodles. When liquid starts to boil, pour over·cornstarch and water mixture. Cook until liquid thickens.

Cucumber and Agar-Agar Salad

COOKING TIME: 40 minutes
CALORIES PER SERVING: 227
PROTEIN PER SERVING: 18.2 g

1 EGG
1 TEASPOON VEGETABLE OIL
1 SMALL CUCUMBER
4 OUNCES CHICKEN BREAST
1 SCALLION CUT INTO 1-INCH PIECES
2 SLICES FRESH GINGER
1 STAR ANISE
6 SZECHUAN PEPPERCORNS
2 SLICES BOILED HAM
⅓ OUNCE DRY SHREDDED AGAR-AGAR
1 TEASPOON DRY CHINESE MUSTARD
    MIXED TO A SMOOTH PASTE WITH HOT
    WATER; LET STAND 10 TO 15 MINUTES
1 TABLESPOON SESAME SEED OIL
1 TABLESPOON RICE VINEGAR
1½ TABLESPOONS SOY SAUCE

1. Beat the egg thoroughly with a pinch of salt. Heat a wok until very hot, brush with a little oil, then turn heat down.

2. Add ½ the egg, and swirl the wok quickly to make 8-inch-diameter thin egg pancake.

3. When surface of pancake starts to dry, transfer to a dish and make another the same way.

4. When pancake sets and is cool enough to handle, slice into julienne strips.

5. Peel and seed cucumber, then shred into 2-inch lengths.

6. Place the chicken breast in a pot. Pour over enough water to just cover the chicken. Add scallion, ginger, star anise, and Szechuan peppercorns. Cover and bring to a boil, then turn the heat to medium and cook for 20 minutes. Drain and cool quickly in cold water. Slice everything into julienne strips.

7. Soak agar-agar in lukewarm water for 10 minutes and drain. Cut into 2-inch pieces.

8. Place cucumber, egg pancake, agar-agar, ham, and chicken on a dish. Combine mustard, sesame seed oil, rice vinegar, and soy sauce. Immediately before serving, pour this mixture over the salad.

1

2

3

4

5

6

7

8

Pickled Cabbage

COOKING TIME: 20 minutes (excluding marinating
time)
CALORIES PER SERVING: 93
PROTEIN PER SERVING: 2.3 g

5 CABBAGE LEAVES
½ STALK CELERY
1 SMALL CARROT
2 TABLESPOONS VINEGAR
2 TABLESPOONS SUGAR
1 TABLESPOON SALT
SOY SAUCE

*SUGGESTIONS: Do not overcook cabbage. If
marinating time is too short, the taste will not
penetrate the cabbage. If you like this dish to be
spicy, you may put hot red pepper powder into the
marinade.*

1. Cook cabbage leaves in boiling water until
tender. Drain and remove as much of main stem as
possible without piercing the leaf.

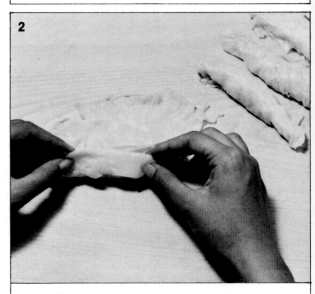

2. Cut celery and carrot into 2-inch-long pieces and
then lengthwise into julienne strips. Place equal
portions carrot and celery on each cabbage leaf.
Roll up tightly, then place in a bowl in 1 layer.

3

3. In a small saucepan, combine vinegar, sugar, and salt. Cook over medium heat until sugar dissolves. Cool and pour over cabbage rolls. Cover the cabbage with plastic wrap.

4

4. Place a small plate into the bowl on top of the plastic-wrapped cabbage, then place either a bowl of water or canned goods on the top of the plate to weigh it down.

5

5. Leave weighted pan at least 2 hours, preferably overnight. When ready to serve, squeeze lightly and cut diagonally into 1-inch pieces. Sprinkle with soy sauce and serve.

Eggs

Black Tea Eggs

COOKING TIME: 40 minutes
CALORIES PER SERVING: 160
PROTEIN PER SERVING: 12.3 g

4 EGGS
1 TABLESPOON BLACK TEA LEAVES
1 STAR ANISE
½ TEASPOON CRUSHED SZECHUAN
   PEPPERCORNS
2 TABLESPOONS SOY SAUCE
¼ TEASPOON SALT
PARSLEY

1. Place eggs in a saucepan, cover with lukewarm water, and bring to a boil. Rolling the eggs with chopsticks or a wooden spoon for 2 to 3 minutes will keep the yolk in the middle of the egg. Cook 10 more minutes. Drain and cool in cold water.

2. Gently tap the eggs with the back of a spoon one at a time to finely crack the shell all over. Do not peel yet.

3. Measure out black tea, star anise, Szechuan peppercorns, soy sauce, and salt.

4. Place the eggs in a wok. Add black tea, star anise, Szechuan peppercorns, soy sauce, and salt. Pour over enough water to just cover the eggs.

5. Cook over medium heat for 20 minutes. Turn off the heat and leave the eggs in the liquid until ready to serve. You may leave in liquid overnight.

6. Drain, discarding everything but the eggs. Cut in half lengthwise and serve with parsley.

Egg and Crabmeat Rolls

COOKING TIME: 40 minutes
CALORIES PER SERVING: 395
PROTEIN PER SERVING: 18.6 g

3 DRIED CHINESE MUSHROOMS
¼ CUP BAMBOO SHOOTS
2 SCALLIONS
½ CUP BEAN SPROUTS
3 TABLESPOONS + ⅔ TEASPOON
   VEGETABLE OIL
¼ POUND OR 1 SMALL CAN OF
   CRABMEAT
½ TEASPOON SALT
1 TEASPOON SOY SAUCE
2 TEASPOONS CORNSTARCH
2 EGGS
3 TABLESPOONS + 1 TEASPOON FLOUR
VEGETABLE OIL FOR DEEP-FRYING
TOMATO KETCHUP
ROASTED SALT AND SZECHUAN
   PEPPERCORNS (SEE PAGE 10)

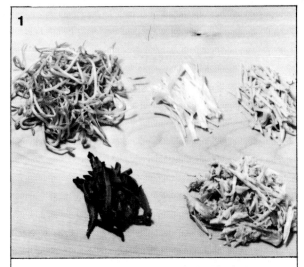

1. Soak mushrooms in warm water for 20 minutes. Drain and remove stems, then shred. Shred bamboo shoots and scallions. Wash bean sprouts in cold water and drain. Heat 3 tablespoons oil in a wok, add scallions, crabmeat, mushrooms, bamboo shoots, and bean sprouts. Stir-fry briefly, then add ¼ teaspoon salt and the soy sauce. Combine cornstarch with 2 tablespoons water, and stir into the wok. Mix thoroughly and remove to a plate. Set aside.

2. Beat the eggs thoroughly with 1 teaspoon flour, 1 tablespoon water, and ¼ teaspoon salt. Divide the egg mixture among 3 small bowls.

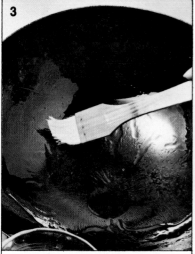

3. Heat a wok until very hot. Brush with a little oil (⅔ teaspoon). Turn the heat low.

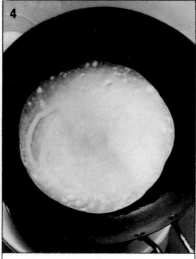

4. Pour 1 bowl of beaten egg into the wok and quickly swirl around to make 6-inch-diameter pancake.

5. When surface of pancake starts to dry, transfer to a plate. In the same manner, make 2 more pancakes.

6. Divide filling evenly into 3 portions and place 1 portion on lower third of each pancake.

7. Roll up tightly halfway. Brush right and left side of pancake with a mixture of 1 tablespoon flour and 3 tablespoons water.

TO STORE COOKING OIL: Strain warm oil into a container which can be tightly closed. Keep the container in refrigerator.

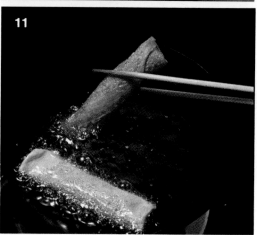

8. Fold right and left sides of pancake toward center, pressing with fingers.

9. Roll up to the end, then seal well with flour and water mixture. Make two more rolls.

10. Heat oil in a wok to 350°. Slip egg rolls into wok, seal side down.

11. Deep-fry the egg rolls until their color turns golden brown. Drain on paper towels. Cut each in 4 and serve with tomato ketchup and roasted salt and Szechuan peppercorns as a dip.

1. Soak dried shrimp in enough warm water to cover for 15 minutes or until they are soft.

2. Drain the shrimp and place on a plate. Sprinkle the sherry over the shrimp and let stand for 3 to 5 minutes.

Scrambled Eggs with Dried Shrimp

COOKING TIME: 25 minutes
CALORIES PER SERVING: 280
PROTEIN PER SERVING: 1 g

2 TABLESPOONS DRIED SHRIMP
1 TEASPOON SHERRY
3 EGGS
½ TEASPOON SALT
3 TABLESPOONS VEGETABLE OIL

NOTE: Shelled and dried shrimp are sold in Chinese groceries. They must be soaked or steamed before using. Dried shrimp will keep stored at room temperature for a few months.

3. In a bowl, beat the eggs thoroughly. Add shrimp and salt. Mix well.

4. Heat oil in a wok. When it is very hot, pour in the egg mixture.

5. Turn the heat to medium. Using a spatula, make soft scrambled eggs. When eggs are cooked, remove from the wok immediately.

Egg Fu Yung (Chinese-Style Omelet)

COOKING TIME: 20 minutes
CALORIES PER SERVING: 495
PROTEIN PER SERVING: 23.1 g

¼ POUND OR 1 SMALL CAN OF CRABMEAT
1 TEASPOON SHERRY
½ TEASPOON MINCED FRESH GINGER
3 EGGS
¼ TEASPOON SALT
3 DRIED CHINESE MUSHROOMS
1 TABLESPOON GREEN PEAS
1 TEASPOON CORNSTARCH
4 TABLESPOONS VEGETABLE OIL
¼ CUP FINELY SHREDDED BAMBOO SHOOTS
1 SCALLION FINELY SHREDDED
½ CUP CHICKEN BROTH

1. Break the crabmeat into small pieces and remove any traces of shell or cartilage. Combine crabmeat with sherry and minced ginger.

2. In a bowl, beat the eggs thoroughly and add crabmeat and salt.

3. Soak the mushrooms in warm water for 20 minutes or until soft. Drain and remove the stems, then shred finely. Cook green peas in boiling, salted water for 1 minute and drain. Mix cornstarch with 1 tablespoon water.

4. Heat 3 tablespoons oil in a wok. When it is very hot pour in the egg mixture.

5. Using a spatula, mix the eggs and push back and forth, then turn them.

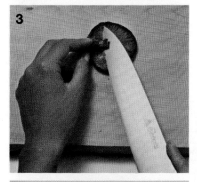

6. Egg should be slightly golden outside yet soft inside. Slip eggs to warm plate. Keep warm until sauce is ready.

7. Clean the wok with paper towels, then heat 1 tablespoon oil in it. Add mushrooms, bamboo shoots, scallion, and green peas. Stir-fry briefly, add chicken broth, and soy sauce. Mix and bring to boil, then stir in cornstarch and water mixture. Cook until liquid thickens. Pour this sauce over the eggs and serve.

Steamed Egg Custard

COOKING TIME: 25 minutes
CALORIES PER SERVING: 214
PROTEIN PER SERVING: 13.8 g

3 EGGS
1½ CUPS CHICKEN BROTH
½ TEASPOON SALT
4 OUNCES SMALL SHRIMP
½ TEASPOON MINCED FRESH GINGER
½ TEASPOON CORNSTARCH
1 TABLESPOON DRIED TREE EARS
½ CUP CANNED SWEET CORN
2 TABLESPOONS VEGETABLE OIL
2 TEASPOONS SOY SAUCE
½ TEASPOON SALT

NOTE: Dried tree ears (cloud ears) are a small
dried fungus, black in color and irregularly shaped.
They are available at Chinese groceries, and must
be soaked in warm water before using. Soaking
makes them swell to 4 to 5 times their dried size.

1. In a large mixing bowl, beat the eggs with a wire whisk. Add chicken broth and salt. Mix thoroughly until liquid is uniformly beaten.

2. Using a spoon, scoop out the bubbles floating over the surface of egg mixture.

3. Heat water in steamer over high heat and bring to boil. Place the egg bowl in steamer and cover tightly. Turn the heat to medium low and cook for about 15 minutes. Stick a knife in the middle of the custard and if clear juice comes up the custard is done. If you are not using a Chinese bamboo steamer, place 2 sheets of paper towel between steamer and cover.

4. Shell and devein the shrimp, then wash and dry with paper towels. Mix shrimp with ginger and ½ teaspoon cornstarch. Set aside. Soak dried tree ears in warm water until they soften. Drain, remove and discard hard part, and break into small pieces. Drain sweet corn. Heat oil in a wok and add shrimp. Stir-fry until shrimp turn pink, then add tree ears and sweet corn. Stir-fry briefly. Add soy sauce and salt. Mix and stir-fry for 1 minute. Place shrimp mixture on top of egg custard and serve.

Bean Curd

Bean Curd with Chili Pepper

COOKING TIME: 15 minutes
CALORIES PER SERVING: 268
PROTEIN PER SERVING: 11.4 g

2 2 × 2 × 1″ SQUARES CHINESE OR 1
   3 × 3 × 2″ SQUARE JAPANESE FRESH
   BEAN CURD
2 DRIED HOT RED PEPPERS (CHILI
   PEPPERS)
1 SCALLION
1 TABLESPOON BEAN PASTE
2 TABLESPOONS SOY SAUCE
1 TEASPOON SUGAR
½ CUP CHICKEN BROTH
3 TABLESPOONS VEGETABLE OIL
½ TEASPOON MINCED GARLIC
4 OUNCES GROUND PORK
2 TEASPOONS CORNSTARCH

1. Cook bean curd in lightly salted water for 2 minutes. Drain on paper towels.

2. Cut the bean curd into ½-inch cubes.

3. Remove the seeds from dried hot red pepper, and chop the scallion, including greens. Combine the bean paste, soy sauce, sugar and chicken broth. Set aside.

4. Heat the oil in a wok, and add dried hot red pepper, scallion, and garlic. Stir-fry briefly, just until garlic is slightly colored.

5. Add ground pork. Mix and stir-fry until pork changes color.

6. Add the bean curd to the wok, and gently mix with the pork.

7. Add bean paste mixture, cover, and bring slowly to a boil. Cook for 3 minutes over medium heat. Mix the cornstarch with 2 tablespoons water and add to the wok. Stir gently until liquid thickens.

NOTE: If soy bean paste cannot be obtained, add 1 more tablespoon of soy sauce as a substitute.

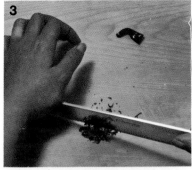

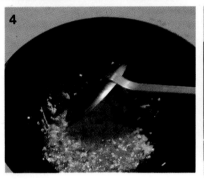

Fresh Bean Curd Salad

COOKING TIME: 15 minutes
CALORIES PER SERVING: 205
PROTEIN PER SERVING: 14.2 g

1 SQUARE JAPANESE FRESH BEAN CURD
  3 × 3 × 2″
¼ CUP SZECHUAN PRESERVED
  KOHLRABI
½ POUND SPINACH
1 TABLESPOON RICE VINEGAR
1½ TABLESPOONS SOY SAUCE
1 TABLESPOON SESAME SEED OIL
¼ CUP MINCED HAM

1. Cook bean curd gently in lightly salted water for 2 minutes. Drain on paper towels. Slice the bean curd in half, then cut into 16 triangles (see photograph). Keep refrigerated until ready to serve.

2. Wash Szechuan preserved kohlrabi under cold water, then soak in cold water for 5 minutes. Remove hard part of stem and mince. Cook the spinach in salted, boiling water until leaves begin to wilt. Drain in cold water, using hands, squeeze the leaves as dry as possible. Chop the spinach.

3. For the dressing, combine rice vinegar, soy sauce, sesame seed oil. Mix well.

4. Mix ham, spinach, and Szechuan preserved kohlrabi and place them in middle of a plate. Arrange chilled bean curd around them. Pour the dressing over all before serving. To eat, break the bean curd with a fork and mix with the vegetables.

Pressed Bean Curd with Pork Shreds

COOKING TIME: 2½ hours
CALORIES PER SERVING: 243
PROTEIN PER SERVING: 15.6 g

1 SQUARE 3 × 3 × 2″ JAPANESE OR 2
  SQUARES 2 × 2 × 1″ FRESH CHINESE
  BEAN CURD
½ TEASPOON SALT
4 OUNCES FRESH PORK
4 TEASPOONS SHERRY
4 TEASPOONS SOY SAUCE
½ TEASPOON CORNSTARCH
4 TABLESPOONS VEGETABLE OIL
½ STALK CELERY
¼ CUP FINELY SHREDDED BAMBOO
  SHOOTS
1 TEASPOON SUGAR

1. Bring 2 cups water to a boil in a
saucepan. Add bean curd and crush into
small pieces with a wire whisk. Reduce heat
to medium. Add ½ teaspoon salt.

2. Drain the bean curd and wrap in cheese
cloth. Squeeze lightly to remove excess
water.

3. Open the cheese cloth on the chopping
board. Using hands, shape bean curd into a
square, then rewrap in cheese cloth, again
shaping into a square. Place a flat board on
top of the bean curd, and put a weight, such
as a large bowl of water or canned goods,
on top of that. Press for 2 hours. Remove the
weight and cheese cloth.

4. Slice the pressed bean curd horizontally,
then cut into 2-inch-long fine shreds. Slice
the pork ⅛-inch thick. Cut the pork into fine
shreds and mix with 1 teaspoon each sherry
and soy sauce, and the cornstarch. Set
aside. Cut celery into 2-inch-long fine
shreds.

5. Heat the oil in a wok and add pork
shreds. Stir-fry until pork changes color,
then add celery, bamboo shoots, and bean
curd. Mix gently and stir-fry. Combine
remaining sherry and soy sauce and sugar.
Add to the wok and mix thoroughly. Stir-fry
for 1 minute.

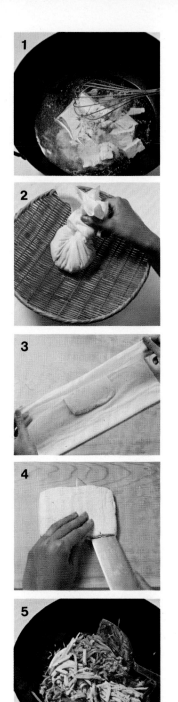

Home-Style Bean Curd

COOKING TIME: 35 minutes
CALORIES PER SERVING: 458
PROTEIN PER SERVING: 13.7 g

8 PUFFED BEAN CURD OR 2 SQUARES
   CHINESE 2 × 2 × 1" FRESH BEAN CURD
4 OUNCES LEAN PORK BUTT
5 TEASPOONS SHERRY
5 TEASPOONS SOY SAUCE
2½ TEASPOONS CORNSTARCH
3 DRIED CHINESE MUSHROOMS
1 GREEN PEPPER
¼ CUP BAMBOO SHOOTS
1 TABLESPOON BEAN PASTE (MISO)
1 TEASPOON SUGAR
4 TABLESPOONS VEGETABLE OIL

*NOTE: To make your own puffed bean curd, drain
the fresh bean curd, pat dry with paper towels, then
quarter each bean curd. Heat ¹⁄₂ cup oil in a wok. Fry
the bean curd pieces in the oil for 4 to 5 minutes on
each side. When both sides are lightly brown,
remove from the wok and drain on paper towels.*

1. Cut the puffed bean curd in half
diagonally to make triangles.

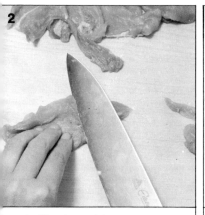

2. Slice the pork into 1-by-1-by-¼-inch pieces and mix with 2 teaspoons each sherry and soy sauce and ½ teaspoon cornstarch. Set aside.

3. Soak mushrooms in warm water for 20 minutes or until soft. Drain, remove the stems, and cut mushrooms into wedges. Cut green pepper in half lengthwise, then remove seeds. Cut the green pepper into 1-inch squares. Cut bamboo shoots into 1-by-1-by-¼-inch slices.

4. Combine bean paste, 1 tablespoon water, 3 teaspoons soy sauce, 3 teaspoons sherry, and the sugar Mix well and set aside. Mix 2 teaspoons cornstarch with 2 tablespoons water.

5. Heat the oil in a wok, add the pork slices. Stir-fry until pork turns color. Add puffed bean curd, bamboo shoots, and mushrooms. Mix, add liquid mixture, and ½ cup water. Bring to boil, reduce heat to medium, and cook for 5 minutes.

6. Add green peppers, cook until green peppers turn bright green. Stir the cornstarch and water mixture into the wok. Mix thoroughly and cook until liquid thickens.

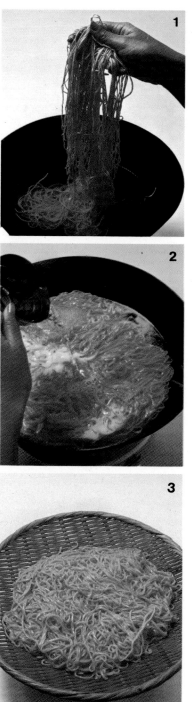

Noodle Soup with Assorted Meats

COOKING TIME: 25 minutes
CALORIES PER SERVING: 669
PROTEIN PER SERVING: 35.3 g

½ POUND FRESH LO MEIN NOODLES
½ CHICKEN BREAST
4 QUAIL EGGS
4 LARGE SHRIMP
2 DRIED CHINESE MUSHROOMS
¼ CUP BAMBOO SHOOTS
10 SNOW PEAS
2 SCALLIONS
2 TABLESPOONS VEGETABLE OIL
4 CUPS CHICKEN BROTH
1 TABLESPOON SOY SAUCE

TO COOK NOODLES (10 minutes):

1. Bring a large quantity of water to a boil in a pot. Separate the noodles by hand and drop into the water.

2. When it returns to a boil, pour in 1 cup of cold water.

3. Bring to a boil again, and boil until the noodles are cooked. Drain immediately.

Noodle Soup with Assorted Meats

SUGGESTIONS: Cook noodles al dente. Warm the serving bowl. Pour the sauce on first before serving.

NOTE: Snow peas are available fresh in any large city with a Chinatown. They are also available frozen, but they are not very crisp. If only frozen snow peas are available, thaw at room temperature, then rinse with cold water. Drain and add to the dish at last minute. Or you may defrost them by submerging in boiling water for just a moment and then rinsing in cold water.

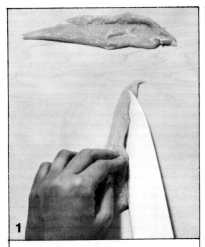

1. Skin and bone the chicken breast.

2. Cut the chicken into bite-size pieces. Hard-boil the quail eggs over simmering water. Cool in cold water and remove the shells.

3. Remove shell and devein the shrimp. Clean under cold water, and dry with paper towels. Split the shrimp and cut into bite-size pieces.

4. Soak mushrooms in warm water for 20 minutes or until soft. Remove stems and cut into wedges. Cut bamboo shoots into bite-size pieces. Remove strings from snow peas. Cut the scallions into 1-inch lengths.

5. Heat the oil in a wok, add scallions, chicken, and shrimp. Stir-fry until their colors change. Add bamboo shoots, mushrooms, and snow peas. Stir a few times and over medium heat, pour in the chicken broth.

6. When the broth starts to boil, add the soy sauce and quail eggs. Place the noodles in 2 warm bowls.

7. Divide chicken, shrimp, and vegetable mixture evenly over the noodles. Pour the soup over filled bowls and serve immediately.

Cold Noodles

COOKING TIME: 25 minutes
CALORIES PER SERVING: 601
PROTEIN PER SERVING: 23.4 g

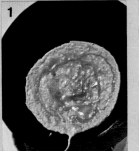

½ CHICKEN BREAST
½ TEASPOON SHERRY
SALT
1 SCALLION, CUT INTO 1-INCH LENGTHS
2 SLICES FRESH GINGER 1½ × 1 × ⅛"
2 TABLESPOONS + 1 TEASPOON SESAME
    SEED OIL
½ CUCUMBER
1 CUP FRESH BEAN SPROUTS
2 TABLESPOONS SESAME SEED PASTE
2 TABLESPOONS SOY SAUCE
2 TABLESPOONS RICE VINEGAR
¼ TEASPOON SUGAR
1 TEASPOON HOT PEPPER OIL
½ POUND FRESH LO MEIN NOODLES
1 EGG

1. Place the chicken on a plate one size smaller than the steamer. Sprinkle the chicken with the sherry and ½ teaspoon salt. Place the scallion and ginger on top of the chicken and steam for 20 minutes. Sprinkle the chicken with 1 teaspoon sesame seed oil. When chicken is cool enough to handle, cut into shreds.

2. Make 2 egg sheets as shown on following page.

3. Peel and seed cucumber, then cut into shreds. Cook bean sprouts just 1 minute in boiling water. Rinse under cold water; drain.

4. In a bowl, mix sesame seed paste with 2 tablespoons water, then add the soy sauce, rice vinegar, sugar, ¼ teaspoon salt, ½ cup water, and the hot pepper oil. Mix well and reserve to use as dressing.

5. Cook the noodles.

6. Place the noodles in 2 plates. Arrange over them the chicken, egg sheets, cucumber shreds, and bean sprouts. When ready to eat, pour the dressing over all and combine.

TO MAKE EGG SHEETS:

For the noodles:

1. Drop ½ pound noodles into 2 to 3 quarts of boiling water and stir to separate them. When water starts to reboil, pour in 1 cup cold water. Cook until centers of noodles are soft.

2. Pour the noodles into a strainer, and rinse under cold water. Drain well.

3. Transfer the noodles to bowl. Mix with 2 tablespoons sesame seed oil.

For the egg sheets:

1. Beat egg thoroughly with pinch of salt. Heat a wok until very hot, then brush the wok with a little oil. Turn the heat to low, and pour in ½ of the beaten egg, and quickly swirl the wok to make a thin even layer. When surface of the egg starts to dry, transfer to a plate. Make 1 more in the same manner.

2. When egg sheets are cool, cut into shreds.

Noodles with Meat Sauce

COOKING TIME: 25 minutes
CALORIES PER SERVING: 755
PROTEIN PER SERVING: 22.9 g

3 TABLESPOONS BEAN PASTE (MISO)
½ TABLESPOON SUGAR
1 TABLESPOON SHERRY
1 TABLESPOON SOY SAUCE
2 SCALLIONS
2 TABLESPOONS VEGETABLE OIL
4 OUNCES GROUND FRESH PORK
½ CUP CHICKEN BROTH OR WATER
1 CUCUMBER
½ POUND FRESH LO MEIN NOODLES
2 TABLESPOONS SESAME SEED OIL

1. Combine bean paste, sugar, sherry, and soy sauce. Mince the scallions. Heat the oil in a wok, add pork and scallions. Stir-fry until pork changes color and dries, and add bean paste mixture and the chicken broth or the water. Turn heat to medium low and cook for 5 minutes.

2. Peel the cucumber and cut in half lengthwise. Remove seeds and shred finely.

3. Cook the noodles as shown on following page.

4. Place the noodles in 2 bowls. When ready to serve, place the sauce and cucumber over the noodles, mix well, and eat.

TO MAKE SAUCE:

1. In a bowl, add 3 tablespoons bean paste (miso), ½ tablespoon sugar, 1 tablespoon each sherry and soy sauce. Mix well until smooth paste. Mince the scallions.

3. Turn the heat to medium low and cook for 5 minutes. Stir occasionally.

2. Heat oil in a wok, add pork and scallions. Stir-fry until pork changes color, and dry. Then add combined sauce and ¼ cup chicken broth or water. Bring to boil.

TO COOK NOODLES:

Drop the noodles in 2 to 3 quarts boiling water and stir to separate them. When water starts to reboil add 1 cup cold water. Cook until center of noodle gets soft, al dente. Drain and rinse under cold water. Drain well. Transfer to the bowl and mix with sesame seed oil.

Pork Chow Mein

COOKING TIME: 25 minutes
CALORIES PER SERVING: 804
PROTEIN PER SERVING: 21.1 g

½ POUND FRESH CHINESE LO MEIN
   NOISE ,
VEGETABLE OIL FOR DEEP-FRYING
   NOODLES
4 OUNCES FRESH PORK BUTT
1 TEASPOON SOY SAUCE
1 TEASPOON + 2 TABLESPOONS
   CORNSTARCH
6 DRIED TREE EARS
1 LEAF CHINESE CELERY CABBAGE
2 SLICES HAM
2 SCALLIONS
3 TABLESPOONS VEGETABLE OIL
1 TEASPOON SHERRY
1 TEASPOON SALT
½ TEASPOON SUGAR
3 CUPS CHICKEN BROTH

*NOTE: The pre-cooked, deep-fried noodles
are available in many Chinese grocery stores.
They save time and effort. If you use these,
begin with step 3.*

1. If you are not using the pre-cooked noodles, drop the uncooked noodles in boiling water and stir to separate. Cook for 1 minute. Rinse under cold water and steam for 10 minutes in a steamer.

2. In a wok, heat to 350° enough oil to cover the noodles. Drop the noodles into oil and deep-fry until crisp. Drain on paper towels.

3. Place the noodles on a plate and cover with paper towels. Press lightly with hand to crush, making noodles easier to eat. Place near the stove to keep warm.

4. Cut the pork into 1-by-1-by-¼-inch pieces, then mix with soy sauce and 1 teaspoon cornstarch.

5. Soak tree ears in warm water until soft. Remove hard part of tree ears and break into small pieces. Cut celery cabbage leaf and ham into 1-inch squares. Cut scallions into 1-inch lengths.

6. Heat oil in a wok, add pork and scallions. Stir-fry until pork changes color. Add celery cabbage, tree ears, and ham. Mix and stir-fry.

7. Add sherry, salt, sugar, and chicken broth. Mix well and cook for 5 minutes. Combine remaining cornstarch with 2 tablespoons water. Add to wok and cook until liquid thickens. Pour over the noodles and serve.

Rice Noodles with Shrimp and Vegetables

COOKING TIME: 20 minutes
CALORIES PER SERVING: 503
PROTEIN PER SERVING: 19.4 g

4 OUNCES DRIED RICE NOODLES
½ CHICKEN BREAST
1½ TEASPOONS FRESH GINGER JUICE
2½ TEASPOONS CORNSTARCH
4 DRIED CHINESE MUSHROOMS
¼ CUP BAMBOO SHOOTS
½ CAN OF ABALONE
4 OUNCES SMALL SHRIMP
2 TABLESPOONS GREEN PEAS
3 TABLESPOONS VEGETABLE OIL
2 TABLESPOONS SHERRY
2 TABLESPOONS SOY SAUCE
½ TEASPOON SALT
1½ CUPS CHICKEN BROTH

NOTE: Rice noodles are fine noodles made from rice flour. They are soaked in lukewarm water before cooking. Rice noodles can be stir-fried, dropped into soups, or deep-fried and served as a garnish. They should not be oversoaked or overcooked, or they will turn into a paste. Serve rice noodles immediately after they finish cooking, otherwise they absorb all liquid and are unpalatable.

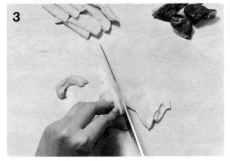

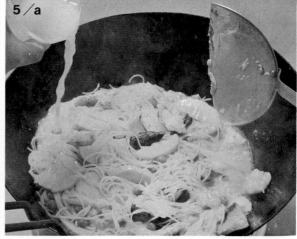

1. Soak the dried rice noodles in lukewarm water for 10 minutes. Drain well.

2. Cut the chicken into bite-size pieces and mix with 1 teaspoon each fresh ginger juice and cornstarch. Set aside.

3. Soak mushrooms in warm water until soft. Remove stems and cut into wedges. Cut bamboo shoots into thin slices. Slice the abalone into thin bite-size pieces. Shell and devein the shrimp. Clean and dry with paper towels. Mix the shrimp with ½ teaspoon each fresh ginger juice and cornstarch. Set aside. Cook green peas in boiling, salted water for 1 minute and drain.

4. Heat oil in a wok, add chicken, shrimp, bamboo shoots, mushrooms, and abalone. Stir-fry until shrimp change color. Add green peas and rice noodles. Stir a few times.

5. Combine the sherry, soy sauce, salt and chicken broth. Add to the wok, mix, and bring to a boil. Mix remaining teaspoon cornstarch with 1 tablespoon water and stir into the wok. Mix thoroughly and cook until liquid thickens.

Dumplings

Pancake with Bean Sauce Dip (Chinese-Style Sandwich with Bean Paste Flavor)

COOKING TIME 3 hours
CALORIES PER SERVING 840
PROTEIN PER SERVING 27.3 g

TO MAKE SAUCE:

1

Recipes for techniques illustrated on right on page 119

TO PREPARE THE PANCAKES.

BEAN SAUCE:

3 OUNCES BEAN PASTE (MISO)
2 TABLESPOONS SUGAR
½ TABLESPOON SOY SAUCE
1 TABLESPOON SHERRY
2 TABLESPOONS VEGETABLE OIL
6 SCALLIONS

PANCAKES:

2 CUPS FLOUR
1 TABLESPOON SESAME SEED OIL
¾ CUP BOILING WATER
1 TABLESPOON VEGETABLE OIL

FILLINGS:

4 OUNCES BOILED OR BAKED HAM
14 OUNCES SMALL SHRIMP
3 TEASPOONS SHERRY
1 TEASPOON CORNSTARCH
8 TABLESPOONS VEGETABLE OIL
2 EGGS
1¾ OUNCES CELLOPHANE NOODLES
1 TEASPOON SOY SAUCE
2 BAKING POTATOES
VEGETABLE OIL FOR DEEP-FRYING
8 OUNCES BEAN SPROUTS

TO MAKE PANCAKES:

1. Place the flour in a large bowl, add sesame seed oil and gradually pour in the boiling water while stirring with chopsticks.

2. When cool enough to handle, knead with your hands for 10 minutes.

3. When dough becomes smooth and silky, cover with a damp cloth and let sit for 15 to 30 minutes.

4. Knead the dough for 2 minutes more and divide into 2 parts. On a lightly floured board, roll each part into a cylinder about 1¼ inches in diameter.

5. Divide each cylinder in 6, to make 12 altogether.

6. Press each cylinder with palm of hand.

TO MAKE PANCAKES:

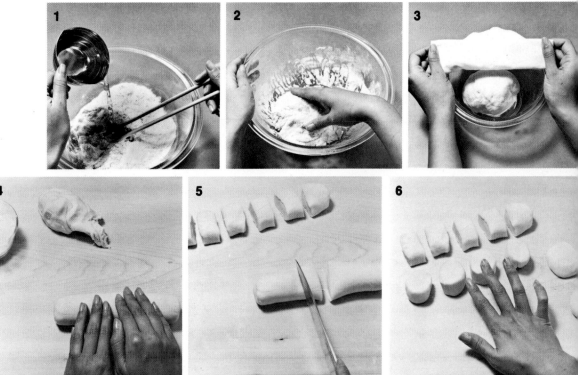

7. Using a rolling pin, evenly roll each piece into circles 3-inches in diameter.

8. Brush the oil lightly and evenly on one side of pancakes. Do not forget to brush oil on edge too, otherwise it will be hard to separate them after cooking.

9. Lay an unoiled pancake on each oiled one. Gently roll each double pancake, working from the center out to make a circle about 6-inches in diameter.

10. Heat an ungreased, heavy frying pan over medium heat. Fry each pancake until surface starts to bubble. Then turn over and fry other side.

11. Remove from the pan, and pull the 2 pancakes apart while still hot. Make 5 more.

12. If you cook pancakes ahead of time, steam until soft in steamer when ready to use.

TO MAKE FILLINGS:

1. Shred the ham into matchstick-size pieces.

2. Shell and devein the shrimp. Wash, drain, and dry with paper towels. Mix the shrimp with 1 teaspoon sherry and cornstarch. Heat 3 tablespoons oil in a wok, add shrimp and stir-fry with pinch of salt until shrimp turn slightly pink.

3. Beat the eggs with pinch of salt. Heat 1 tablespoon oil in a wok. Scramble the eggs in the wok.

4. Soak the cellophane noodles in lukewarm water for 10 minutes. Drain and cut into 4-inch lengths. Heat 2 tablespoons oil in a wok. Add cellophane noodles and soy sauce. Stir-fry for 1 minute.

5. Peel the potatoes and cut into matchstick shreds. Heat deep-frying oil in a wok. When it is hot, drop in potatoes and deep-fry until they turn golden brown and crisp. Drain on paper towels, and sprinkle with salt.

6. Wash and drain the bean sprouts. Heat 2 tablespoons oil in a wok, add bean sprouts. Stir-fry brieflyand add remaining 2 teaspoons sherry and salt to taste. Place each filling in separate, small serving dishes and serve with bean sauce and scallions.

Illustrations for preparing recipes below on pages 116 and 117.

TO MAKE SAUCE:

1. Combine bean paste (miso), sugar, soy sauce, and sherry. Heat oil in a wok, add sauce, and stir until sauce warms. Pour sauce into a small dish and set aside. It is ready for use.

2. Using white part only of scallions, cut into 2-inch lengths. With the sharp point of knife, make lengthwise slits about ¾ inch long on one end. Place them in a bowl of ice water until cut parts curl like flowers.

TO PREPARE THE PANCAKES:

1. Spread a pancake on a plate, dip the scallion in the sauce and brush the center part of the pancake with it. The scallion is then placed in the middle of pancake with small bits of each ingredient.

2. The pancake is folded over the scallion and other filling and tucked under them. Fold right and left side of corner and roll up the pancake to make a cylinder. Eat with your fingers.

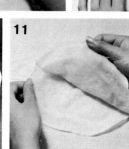

Shao Mai (Steamed Crabmeat and Pork Dumplings)

COOKING TIME: 40 minutes
CALORIES PER SERVING: 653
PROTEIN PER SERVING: 22.5 g

¼ POUND OR 1 SMALL CAN CRABMEAT
½ ONION
25 GREEN PEAS
4 OUNCES FRESH GROUND PORK
1 TABLESPOON SHERRY
1 TABLESPOON SOY SAUCE
¾ TABLESPOON SALT
1 TEASPOON SUGAR
1 TABLESPOON CORNSTARCH
1 TABLESPOON SESAME SEED OIL
25 SHEETS SHAO MAI OR WONTON
   WRAPPERS
RICE VINEGAR, HOT MUSTARD, SOY
   SAUCE AS DIPS

SUGGESTION: Instead of using ground pork and crabmeat you may use one or the other as a filling. Double the pork or crabmeat: pork filling, 8 ounces ground pork; crabmeat filling, ½ pound or 2 small cans. Other ingredients are the same. When you make shao mai ahead of time, do not steam until ready to serve. Keep shao mai in refrigerator covered with damp cloth.

1. Remove crab cartilage, and break into small pieces. Mince the onion. Cook green peas in boiling, salted water for 1 minute and drain.

2. In a bowl combine the pork, crabmeat, onion, sherry, soy sauce, salt, sugar, cornstarch, and sesame seed oil. Mix well to make filling.

3. Place about 1 tablespoon of filling in the center of each wrapper. As each dumpling is finished, cover with a damp cloth to prevent drying.

4. Fold the 4 corners of wrapper over filling.

5. Place the shao mai between thumb and forefinger, and gently squeeze the middle to make sure the wrapper sticks firmly against the filling.

6. Press top and bottom lightly with other hand so that shao mai can stand with the filling exposed at the top.

7. Place 1 green pea on top of each shao mai, and press lightly.

8. Brush the steamer with a little oil. You may use wax paper instead of brushing with oil.

9. Place the shao mai in the steamer, leaving a little space between each shao mai. Cover and steam for 15 minutes. If you are not using a Chinese bamboo steamer, place a cheesecloth between steamer and cover. Cover tightly. This prevents water from dropping into shao mai during steaming.

10. Serve directly from the steamer. Serve hot mustard, soy sauce, and vinegar as dips.

Steamed Buns with Sweet Red Bean and Ground Pork Fillings

COOKING TIME: 2 hours
CALORIES PER SERVING: 180 (meat), 237 (bean)
PROTEIN PER SERVING: 4.9 g (meat), 6.7 g (bean)

SWEET RED BEAN FILLING:
2 CUPS RED BEANS
1 CUP SUGAR
1 TABLESPOON SESAME PASTE
RED FOOD COLORING

MEAT FILLING:
1 LEAF CHINESE CELERY CABBAGE
2 DRIED CHINESE MUSHROOMS
½ CUP SHRIMP
4 OUNCES FRESH GROUND PORK
⅓ TEASPOON GRATED FRESH GINGER
1 TABLESPOON MINCED SCALLION
1½ TABLESPOONS SESAME SEED OIL
1 TABLESPOON SHERRY
1 TABLESPOON SOY SAUCE
⅓ TEASPOON SALT
½ TEASPOON SUGAR

DOUGH:
1 TABLESPOON DRY YEAST
2 TEASPOONS SUGAR (FOR YEAST)
2 TABLESPOONS FLOUR (FOR YEAST)
½ CUP LUKEWARM WATER (FOR YEAST)
5 CUPS FLOUR
½ TEASPOON SALT
1 TABLESPOON SUGAR
1½ CUPS LUKEWARM WATER

TO MAKE MEAT FILLING:

1. Finely chop the celery cabbage. Soak mushrooms in warm water until soft, about 20 minutes. Drain and chop. Shell the shrimp and devein. Chop finely.

2. In a bowl combine pork, ginger, celery cabbage, scallion, mushroom, shrimp, and sesame seed oil. Add sherry, soy sauce, salt, sugar. Using hands, mix well until meat holds together. Divide into 8 portions. Make filling while dough is rising.

TO MAKE SWEET RED BEAN FILLING:

1. Wash red beans in cold water and drain. Place them in a pot with enough cold water to cover. Cook until centers of the beans are soft. Drain and discard cooking liquid. Using a wooden spoon, push the beans through a fine sieve. (You may also use a food mill or electric blender to make this puree).

2. In a wok or saucepan, combine bean puree, sugar, sesame paste, and salt to taste. Stirring, cook over medium heat until smooth and silky, then divide into 8 portions.

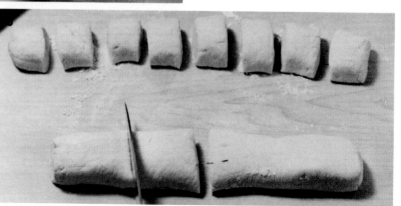

TO MAKE YEAST DOUGH:

1. In a small bowl, combine dry yeast, 2 teaspoons sugar, 2 tablespoons flour, and ½ cup lukewarm water. Mix thoroughly and let stand in warm place for about 20 minutes, or until surface starts to bubble.

2. Place flour in a large bowl. Add salt, sugar, and yeast. Stirring with 4 chopsticks, pour lukewarm water gradually into the bowl. Knead several times with hands.

3. Transfer the dough onto a lightly floured board and knead until smooth.

4. Replace the dough in the large bowl. Cover with a damp cloth and let rise in a warm place for 1 to 2 hours, or until doubled in bulk.

5. Transfer the dough onto the board again and knead for 10 minutes or until dough is smooth.

6. Using both hands, roll the dough into a cylinder, 2 inches in diameter. Cut the roll in half, then cut each half into 8 portions, to make 16 buns altogether. Cover the buns with damp cloth until ready to fill.

TO WRAP FILLING:

1. With the palm of your hand, flatten each bun into a circle. At this step the dough dries easily, so keep under the damp cloth.

2. With a small rolling pin, roll each bun into a 4-inch disk. The center of the disk should be thicker than the edge.

3. Place ⅛ of meat filling in the center of each disk. Gather the edge of the disk together to form a pouch by making pleats.

4. Using the thumb and forefinger, pinch each pleat to seal the bun. Make 7 more in this same manner.

5. Repeat the filling operation with the red bean filling. Turn the buns upside down and shape round. (Seal side should be at the bottom.) Make a dot with red food coloring to distinguish sweet from salty buns.

TO STEAM:

1. Place wax paper or a damp cloth at the bottom of steamer, then set each finished bun on the wax paper or damp cloth. Leave a little space between them. Cover and place in a warm place for 30 minutes for buns to rise.

2. Bring water to a boil. Place the steamer over the boiling water and steam the buns over high heat for 15 to 20 minutes. Do not open the cover while steaming. You may use 2 tiers of the steamer.

12 Fried Dumplings

COOKING TIME: 1½ hours
CALORIES PER SERVING: 117 per dumpling
PROTEIN PER SERVING: 2.2 g per dumpling

FILLINGS:

6 OUNCES CABBAGE
4 OUNCES FRESH GROUND PORK
1 TEASPOON MINCED SCALLION
½ TEASPOON GRATED FRESH GINGER
⅓ TEASPOON SALT
1½ TABLESPOONS SOY SAUCE
1 TEASPOON SHERRY
1½ TABLESPOONS SESAME SEED OIL

DOUGH:

1½ CUPS FLOUR
½ CUP HOT WATER

SAUCE:

2 TABLESPOONS VEGETABLE OIL
½ CUP HOT WATER
HOT CHILI PEPPER OIL
SOY SAUCE
VINEGAR

NOTE: Dumplings can be steamed for 15 minutes.
Boiled dumplings are kneaded with half amount
boiled water as flour and cooked in boiling water for
12 to 13 minutes and served in hot water in which
dumplings are boiled.

1. Shred the cabbage. Cook in boiling salted water for 1 minute and drain. Mince the cabbage, and place it in a cheesecloth and squeeze out excess water.

2. In a bowl, combine pork, cabbage, scallion, ginger, salt, soy sauce, sherry, and sesame seed oil. Mix well, until meat holds together. Set aside.

3. Place the flour in another bowl. Stirring with chopsticks, gradually pour the hot water into the flour.

4. When cool enough to handle, transfer onto lightly floured board and knead with your hands until smooth but firm.

5. Put the dough back in the bowl, and cover with a damp cloth. Let stand for 15 to 20 minutes.

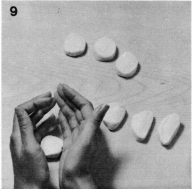

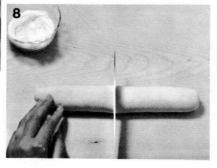

6. Turn the dough onto lightly floured board again and knead 5 minutes more.

7. Using your hands, roll the dough into a cylinder about 1¼ inches in diameter.

8. Cut long sausagelike cylinder in half, then cut each half in 6, to make 12 pieces altogether.

9. Place the pieces, cut sides down, on the board and dust lightly with flour.

10. With the palm of hand, press each piece into a flat circle. Using a small rolling pin, roll each piece into a disk, about 3 to 4 inches in diameter. Hold the piece in your left hand, and turn rolling pin clockwise with your right hand to roll and keep the shape round and the edges thinner than the center.

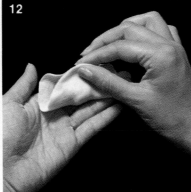

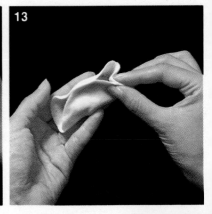

11. Place $^1/_{12}$ of filling in the center of each wrapper.

12. Fold the dough in half to cover the filling.

13. Starting from right side, pinch the edge of dough.

14. Push the extra dough edge around to the back to make pleats between right edge and center.

15. Pinch left edge of dough and make pleats with extra dough between left edge and the center.

16. Press and seal the openings with your thumb and forefinger. Shape dumplings into half moon shape.

17. Heat oil in a wok, and arrange uncooked dumplings in one layer.

18. Cover and fry until bottoms of dumplings turn light brown.

19. Add 4 tablespoons hot water, cover, and turn the heat to medium. Cook until the water has been absorbed by dumplings. Transfer the dumplings to serving plate, brown side up, and serve with hot chili pepper oil and soy sauce and vinegar mixture as a dip.

Fried Shrimp Wontons

COOKING TIME: 25 minutes
CALORIES PER SERVING: 383
PROTEIN PER SERVING: 19.4 g

6 OUNCES SMALL SHRIMP
1 TABLESPOON SHERRY
1 TABLESPOON MINCED SCALLION
½ TABLESPOON FRESH GINGER JUICE
½ TEASPOON SALT
1½ TABLESPOONS CORNSTARCH
30 WONTON SHEETS (AVAILABLE AT
    ORIENTAL FOOD SHOPS)
VEGETABLE OIL FOR DEEP-FRYING
1 TABLESPOON TOMATO KETCHUP
1 TABLESPOON SUGAR
1 TEASPOON VINEGAR

NOTE: One can enjoy fried wontons as an hors d'oeuvre, hot or cold, with or without sauce, and also in soups. When you deep-fry the wontons, do not let the oil temperature get too high, or wrapper will burn but filling will be uncooked.

1. Shell and devein the shrimp. Wash, drain, and dry with paper towels, then mince. In a bowl, combine minced shrimp, sherry, scallion, ginger juice, salt, and 1 tablespoon cornstarch. Mix well to make filling. Cover the wonton wrappers with a damp cloth while wrapping to prevent them from drying out. Have beside you ½ cup cold water in a small bowl. Place 1 teaspoon filling in the center of each wrapper. Dip your finger in the water, and moisten the edge of the wrapper.

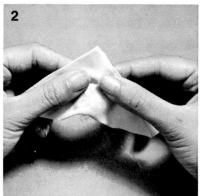

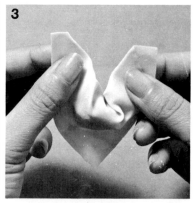

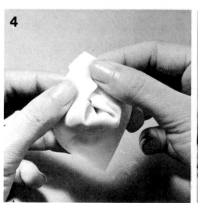

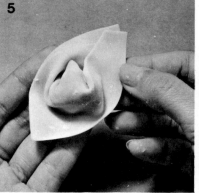

2. Fold the wrapper in half to make a triangle. Pinch all around to seal in the filling.

3. Face the top of the triangle down and take right and left ends in the fingers of both hands.

4. Pull the ends toward each other until the ends meet and overlap.

5. Pinch the ends tightly together to seal. Make 30 wontons.

6. Heat oil in a wok over medium heat. When it is hot, drop 8 wontons at a time into the oil.

7. Deep-fry for 3 to 4 minutes or until crisp. Drain on paper towels. In a small saucepan, combine tomato ketchup, sugar, ¼ teaspoon salt, vinegar, remaining ½ tablespoon cornstarch, and 6 cup water. Stir and bring to boil to make sauce. Place the wontons on the serving plate and pour the sauce over them and serve.

Rice

Chicken Rice Congee

COOKING TIME: 1 hour, 20 minutes
CALORIES PER SERVING: 210
PROTEIN PER SERVING: 15.1 g

½ CUP UNCOOKED WHITE RICE
4 OUNCES BONED CHICKEN BREAST
2 DRIED CHINESE MUSHROOMS
4 OUNCES BOK CHOY OR LETTUCE
1 TEASPOON FRESH GINGER JUICE
2 TEASPOONS SHERRY
1 TEASPOON SALT

1. Wash and drain the rice and let stand for 30 minutes.

2. Remove the skin from the chicken and cut the meat into ½-inch cubes.

3. Soak mushrooms in warm water for 20 minutes or until soft. Drain and remove the stems, then cut into ½-inch squares.

4. Wash and drain bok choy. Cut stalk and leaves into ½-inch pieces. Place the drained rice in heavy saucepan and add 2½ cups of water. Cover and bring to boil.

5. Turn the heat to low, and continue cooking for 40 minutes. Add chicken, mushrooms, bok choy, ginger juice, sherry, and salt. Cook 10 minutes more or until water thickens and the rice grains become very soft. Serve in saucepan or transfer to a warm serving bowl.

Ham and Egg
Fried Rice

COOKING TIME: 25 minutes
CALORIES PER SERVING: 757
PROTEIN PER SERVING: 19.3 g

¼ CUP BAMBOO SHOOTS
2 SLICES COOKED HAM
2 DRIED CHINESE MUSHROOMS
2 SCALLIONS
3 SHRIMP
2 EGGS
5 TABLESPOONS VEGETABLE OIL
2 TABLESPOONS COOKED GREEN PEAS
   (FRESH OR FROZEN)
1½ CUPS COLD COOKED RICE

*NOTE: Fried rice is considered a simple recipe,
and it can be if you understand certain basic rules:
All the ingredients should be cut uniformly so they
are cooked simultaneously. Heat the wok before
adding oil, then add the ingredients. This prevents
finished dish from being greasy. Be careful in
stirring the rice not to break the kernels.*

*SUGGESTION: Chinese roast pork can be
substituted for the ham.*

1. Place the cold cooked rice in a bowl. Gently separate into smaller chunks, using fork or wooden spatula.

2. Cut the bamboo shoots and the ham into ⅓-inch-square cubes.

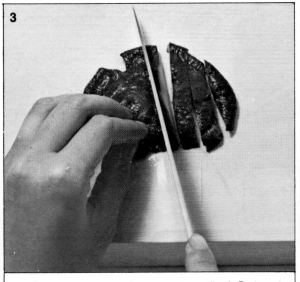

3. Soak the mushrooms in warm water until soft. Drain and cut into ⅓-inch-square pieces.

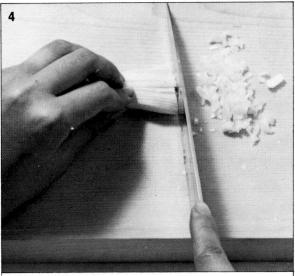

4. Mince the scallions. Shell and devein the shrimp. Wash and drain, then cook in boiling water. Drain and cut each into 4 or 5 pieces.

5. In a bowl, thoroughly beat eggs with pinch of salt. Heat 2 tablespoons oil in a wok, add beaten eggs and scramble until eggs have a soft consistency. Dish out and set aside. Wipe the wok clean with paper towels.

6. In the wok, heat 1 tablespoon oil, add scallions, bamboo shoots, ham, mushrooms, and green peas. Stir-fry briefly and remove to another dish.

COOKED RICE: Rice should be cooked and cold because hot rice will become sticky. When cooking the rice for this recipe, use less water than usual for boiled rice.

7. Wipe the wok with paper towels and heat over high heat until very hot. Add 2 tablespoons oil and swirl to coat the wok. Add the rice.

8. Stir-fry the rice until hot and the kernels separate.

9. Add all ingredients except eggs. Mix well with the rice. Add the scrambled eggs, stirring to mix well.

10. Add ½ teaspoon salt and ¼ teaspoon pepper. Stir once more and remove from the heat. Serve hot.

Chicken Soup with Szechuan Preserved Kohlrabi

COOKING TIME: 15 minutes
CALORIES PER SERVING: 155
PROTEIN PER SERVING: 21.2 g

6 OUNCES BONED CHICKEN BREAST
1 TABLESPOON + 2 TEASPOONS SHERRY
1½ TEASPOONS SOY SAUCE
½ TEASPOON CORNSTARCH
2 TABLESPOONS SZECHUAN PRESERVED
   PICKLES
¼ CUP BAMBOO SHOOTS

*SUGGESTIONS: Do not use any salt since
Szechuan preserved pickles are salty, even if
washed before cooking. Do not cook too long after
vegetables are added or vegetables will lose their
crisp texture.*

1. Cut the chicken breast into bite-size pieces and place them in a bowl. Add 1 tablespoon sherry, 1 teaspoon soy sauce, and cornstarch to the chicken. Mix and let stand for 10 minutes. This marination will give soup a better taste.

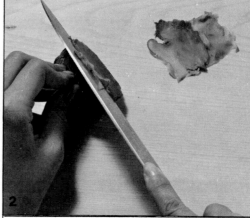

2. Wash Szechuan preserved pickles under running cold water. Dry with paper towels, and slice into thin pieces, then shred.

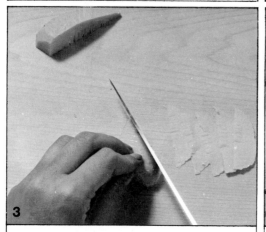

3. Slice bamboo shoots into thin pieces, then shred. Bring 3 cups of water to a boil, then add ½ teaspoon soy sauce and 2 teaspoons sherry.

4. Add chicken pieces to the water and cook until chicken turns white. Add bamboo shoots and Szechuan preserved pickles. When soup boils again, remove from heat and serve in warm soup bowls.

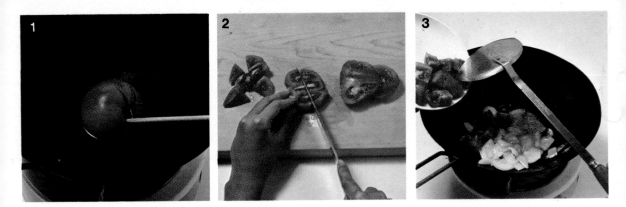

Tomato and Egg Flower Soup

COOKING TIME: 15 minutes
CALORIES PER SERVING: 210
PROTEIN PER SERVING: 1.8 g

2 SMALL TOMATOES
½ ONION
3 TABLESPOONS VEGETABLE OIL
½ TEASPOON SALT
½ TEASPOON SHERRY
1 EGG
1 TABLESPOON MINCED PARSLEY

1. Drop the tomatoes for 30 seconds to 1 minute in boiling water, then cool in cold water.

2. Remove the stems and peel the tomatoes. Slice them ½-inch thick, then cut the slices into 1-inch-square pieces. Drain lightly and set aside.

3. Cut the onion into 1-inch pieces. Heat oil in a wok. Add onion and stir-fry until pieces are transparent. Add tomato pieces. Stir-fry gently (not to break the tomatoes). Add 3 cups of water.

4. When water starts to boil add salt, sherry, and a sprinkling of pepper. Beat the egg thoroughly, and pour into soup.

5. As soon as the soup boils again, remove from the heat and stir briefly with chopsticks. Add parsley and serve in warm soup bowls.

Celery Cabbage Soup

COOKING TIME: 25 minutes
CALORIES PER SERVING: 495
PROTEIN PER SERVING: 13.2 g

2 SCALLIONS
10 OUNCES CELERY CABBAGE
4 OUNCES FRESH LEAN PORK BUTT
2 TABLESPOONS SHERRY
1 TEASPOON SOY SAUCE
1 TEASPOON CORNSTARCH
1¾ OUNCES DRIED CELLOPHANE
    NOODLES
2 TABLESPOONS VEGETABLE OIL
2 SLICES FRESH GINGER
5 CUPS CHICKEN BROTH
1 TEASPOON SALT

NOTE: You may serve this as a main dish.

1. Slice the scallions into very thin pieces crosswise.

2. Cut celery cabbage lengthwise in 3's, then make 2 or 3 diagonal cuts crosswise.

3. Slice the pork into pieces ¼-inch thick. Place the pork slices in a bowl with 1 tablespoon sherry, the soy sauce, cornstarch, and a pinch of salt. Mix and let stand for 2 to 3 minutes.

4. Soak the cellophane noodles in lukewarm water until partly soft, about 15 to 20 minutes. Drain and set aside. (Do not soak cellophane noodles in boiling hot water.)

5. Heat oil in a wok, add scallions, ginger, and pork. Stir-fry briefly, then add chicken broth and celery cabbage. Bring to a boil and simmer for about 10 minutes over medium heat.

6. Add cellophane noodles, 1 tablespoon sherry, salt, and pepper. Remove from heat as soon as soup returns to the boil after adding cellophane noodles, or the noodles will turn to starch. Serve in warm soup bowls.

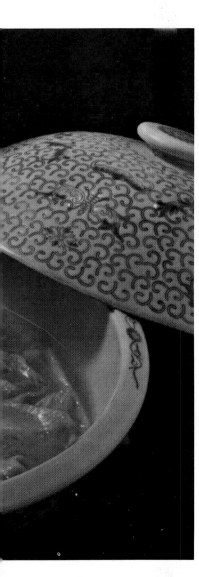

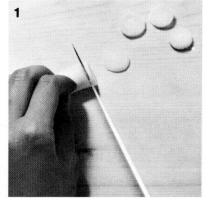

Velvet Corn Soup

COOKING TIME: 10 minutes
CALORIES PER SERVING: 250
PROTEIN PER SERVING: 10.6 g

2 THIN SLICES HAM
2½ CUPS WATER OR CHICKEN BROTH,
  OR WATER AND CHICKEN BROTH
  MIXED
1 CUP CANNED CREAMED CORN
1 TABLESPOON CORNSTARCH
1 EGG

NOTE: You may substitute minced parsley for the ham.

1. Mince the ham slices. Bring chicken broth or water to a boil and add corn. Do not add corn before water starts to boil.

2. Mix cornstarch with 3 tablespoons water and add to the soup. Mix thoroughly.

3. In a small bowl, beat the egg thoroughly.

4. When soup thickens and boils again, slowly pour in the beaten egg. Stir a few times and remove from heat. Serve in warm bowls, sprinkled with minced ham.

TO MAKE CLEAR CHICKEN STOCK
  (4 TO 5 CUPS):

1. Wash the bones of 1 whole chicken under cold running water, then place in large bowl. Add enough cold water to cover. Soak for 30 minutes.

2. In a deep pot, add chicken bones, 8 cups of cold water, 1 or 2 slices of fresh ginger and 2 scallions cut into 1-inch lengths. Cook over medium heat without cover.

3. When water comes to a boil remove scum which floats to the surface. Turn the heat to low and simmer for 2 hours. Remove scum a few times.

4. Slowly and gently pour the stock into a bowl and let cool.

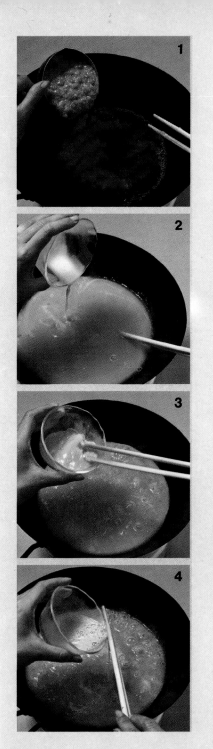

Fish Soup

COOKING TIME: 25 minutes
CALORIES PER SERVING: 252
PROTEIN PER SERVING: 21.6 g

6 OUNCES FILLET OF FLOUNDER, SOLE,
  OR ANY FIRM WHITE FISH
1 EGG
2 TABLESPOONS SHERRY
1½ TEASPOONS CORNSTARCH
1½ TEASPOONS FLOUR
VEGETABLE OIL FOR DEEP-FRYING
½ CUCUMBER
5 CANNED MUSHROOMS
½ TEASPOON SALT
1 TEASPOON FRESH GINGER JUICE

SUGGESTION: To make clear soup, deep-fry the
fish until it is just slightly colored, not brown. You
may use fish balls instead of fish pieces. With
cleaver or meatgrinder, make a fine paste of the fish
fillets, adding 1 tablespoon sherry and 1½
teaspoons cornstarch. Mix very well and make
bite-size balls. Deep-fry.

1. Remove any skin from the fish and cut
into bite-size pieces.

1

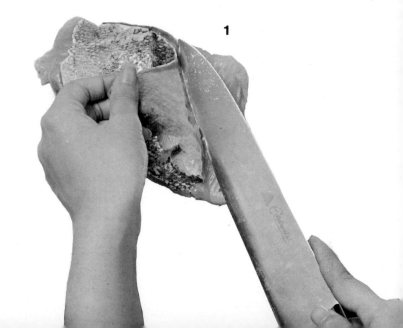

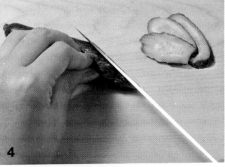

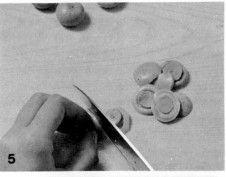

2. Beat the egg in a bowl. Add fish pieces, 1 tablespoon sherry, cornstarch, and flour. Mix well.

3. Heat oil in a wok over medium heat. When oil is hot, drop in the fish pieces a few at a time, and deep-fry until fish colors slightly. Do not allow the oil temperature to get too high or fish will brown and cloud the soup. If you drop too many fish pieces in the oil at any time, the oil temperature drops and fish becomes greasy.

4. Wash the cucumber and slice very thin.

5. Slice the mushrooms ⅛-inch thick.

6. Heat 2½ cups water in a pot over medium heat. When water starts to boil, drop the fish pieces gently into the water.

7. Add cucumbers, mushrooms, 1 tablespoon sherry, salt, a pinch of pepper, and fresh ginger juice. Mix gently. As soon as soup begins to boil, remove from heat and serve in warm bowls.

Pot Dishes

Genghis Khan Barbeque

COOKING TIME: 30 minutes
CALORIES PER SERVING: 665
PROTEIN PER SERVING: 44 g

14 OUNCES BONELESS LEAN LAMB
½ LEMON, THINLY SLICED
2 TABLESPOONS SHERRY
2 TABLESPOONS SOY SAUCE
1 TEASPOON GRATED FRESH GINGER
2 LARGE SHRIMP
¼ POUND SPINACH
1 BUNCH CHINESE CHIVES
10 DRIED CHINESE MUSHROOMS
1 SWEET RED PEPPER
2 SWEET GREEN PEPPERS
1 ONION
4 OUNCES PORK FAT

FOR THE DIP:

2 TABLESPOONS CHINESE WHITE TURNIP
1 TABLESPOON GRATED FRESH GINGER
2 CLOVES GARLIC
2 SCALLIONS
2 TEASPOONS HOT CHILI PEPPER

TO MAKE DIP:

Peel and grate turnip, ginger, and garlic.
Mince the scallions. Place these dip
ingredients and hot chili pepper in small
separate bowls:

a. grated Chinese white turnip

b. minced scallion

c. grated ginger

d. hot chili pepper

e. grated garlic

1. Wash and drain the shrimp. Remove the legs but leave shell and tail on. Wash and drain the spinach and cut into 3-inch lengths. Cut the Chinese chives into 4-inch lengths.

2. Soak the mushrooms in warm water for 20 minutes and drain. Remove the stems. Core and seed green and red peppers and quarter them lengthwise. Slice the onion ¼-inch thick.

3. Arrange shrimp, spinach, Chinese chives, red and green peppers, and onion on a large plate. Put on the table along with the lamb.

4. Put the 5 various dip bowls plus a bowl of soy sauce and a bowl of sherry on the table.

5. Heat the pan over medium heat until very hot and rub the surface with pork fat until well coated. Put the lamp, shrimp, and vegetables in the pan and cook. Keep the surface well greased while cooking. Meanwhile, each person mixes his dip in his own bowl from the various dips on the table. Cooked ingredients are dipped into individual sauce bowls and eaten while hot.

TO MARINATE THE LAMB:

1. Slice the lamb into bite-size pieces.

2. In a baking dish, arrange the lamb slices in 1 layer. Place the lemon slices on top. In a bowl combine sherry, soy sauce, and grated ginger. Pour over the lamb and let stand for 10 minutes, turning the meat a few times.

This recipe calls for a particular kind of iron pan (Korean Grill) which can be purchased in Oriental food stores in the United States.
You can, however, substitute a heavy iron saucepan. The pan should be heated to very hot and then rubbed with pork fat before putting in ingredients.

Chinese Fire Pot

COOKING TIME: 40 minutes
CALORIES PER SERVING: 740
PROTEIN PER SERVING: 34.2 g

½ WHOLE CHICKEN BREAST
2 SCALLIONS CUT INTO 1-INCH LENGTHS
1 SLICE FRESH GINGER 1 × 1½ × ⅛″
5 OUNCES GROUND PORK
4 TABLESPOONS MINCED SCALLION
2 TABLESPOONS MINCED FRESH GINGER
½ BEATEN EGG
1 TEASPOON CORNSTARCH
SALT
1 TEASPOON + 1 TABLESPOON SHERRY
VEGETABLE OIL FOR DEEP-FRYING
8 DRIED CHINESE SHRIMP
2 OUNCES HAM
2 OUNCES DRIED CELLOPHANE
   NOODLES
1 OUNCE SNOW PEAS
4 DRIED CHINESE MUSHROOMS
50 BAMBOO SHOOTS
4 CHINESE CELERY CABBAGE LEAVES
HOT CHILI PEPPER OIL, SOY SAUCE, RICE
   VINEGAR FOR DIPPING
4-6 EGGS

NOTE: The Chinese fire pot is a unique cooking and serving utensil, popular for winter cooking. It is made of metal, usually copper or brass. There is a base and chimney for charcoal. Make sure the charcoal is completely afire before cooking. Today electric fire pots are available. For the fire pot you can substitute a heavy saucepan, Dutch oven, or casserole. In addition to the ingredients given here, thinly sliced, lean pork or canned abalone can be used.

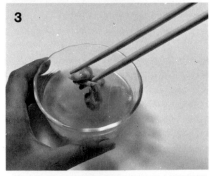

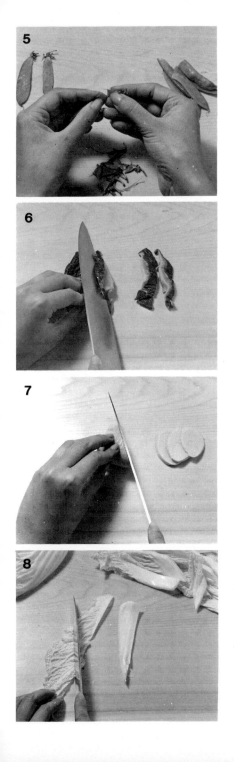

1. Place the chicken in a deep pot. Add 4 cups hot water, 1-inch scallion pieces, and the ginger slice. Bring to boil and simmer until chicken is cooked, removing scum as necessary. Remove the chicken from the pot. Strain the cooking liquid and save. When the chicken is cool enough to handle, remove the bone carefully and cut the chicken into bite-size pieces.

2. In a bowl, mix the ground pork with 1 tablespoon each minced scallion and ginger, ½ beaten egg, cornstarch, ¼ teaspoon salt, and sherry. Mix very well and make 8 meatballs. Heat oil over medium heat, and deep-fry the meatballs. Drain.

3. Soak the dried shrimp in lukewarm water until soft; drain. Slice the ham into 1-by-2-by-¼-inch pieces.

4. Cut the cellophane noodles into 3-inch lengths and soak in lukewarm water for 15 minutes; drain.

5. String and wash the snow peas and cook in boiling, salted water for 30 seconds. Rinse under cold water.

6. Soak the mushrooms in warm water until soft; drain. Remove the stems and cut the caps into ½-inch strips.

7. Slice the bamboo shoots ¼-inch thick.

8. Cut the cerlery cabbage lengthwise into 1½-inch-wide pieces, then cut each lengthwise piece diagonally into 2 or 3 pieces.

9. Sprinkle remaining 3 tablespoons minced scallions and 1 tablespoon minced ginger in the bottom of the fire pot.

10. Sprinkle the shrimp over them, and place the celery cabbage on top of the shrimp. Place the cellophane noodles on top of the cabbage.

11. Partly overlapping, arrange meatballs, snow peas, bamboo shoots, ham, chicken, and mushrooms in the pot (see picture).

12. Add enough water to the reserved chicken liquid to make 5 cups. Add 2 teaspoons salt and 2 tablespoons sherry to the liquid. Gently pour enough liquid into the pot to just cover the ingredients. Reserve balance of the liquid and add if necessary during cooking.

13. Cover the pot and carefully, with tongs, place hot charcoal in the chimney and cook. When the food is ready to eat, the ingredients are placed in individual bowls, and eaten while hot, using one's favorite dip, such as soy sauce, rice vinegar, hot chili pepper oil, or a mixture of these.

14. When most of the food is eaten, break the eggs into the broth, making a tasty, hot soup. When dinner is done, place a small bowl of water on top of the chimney to put out the fire.

Desserts

Almond Curd

COOKING TIME: 40 minutes
CALORIES PER SERVING: 119
PROTEIN PER SERVING: 2.5 g

2 PACKAGES UNFLAVORED GELATIN OR
  ½ STICK AGAR-AGAR
2½ CUPS WATER
4 TABLESPOONS CONDENSED MILK
1 TEASPOON ALMOND EXTRACT
1 CUP WATER ⎫
⅓ CUP SUGAR ⎬ FOR SYRUP
12 SEEDLESS GRAPES, PEELED

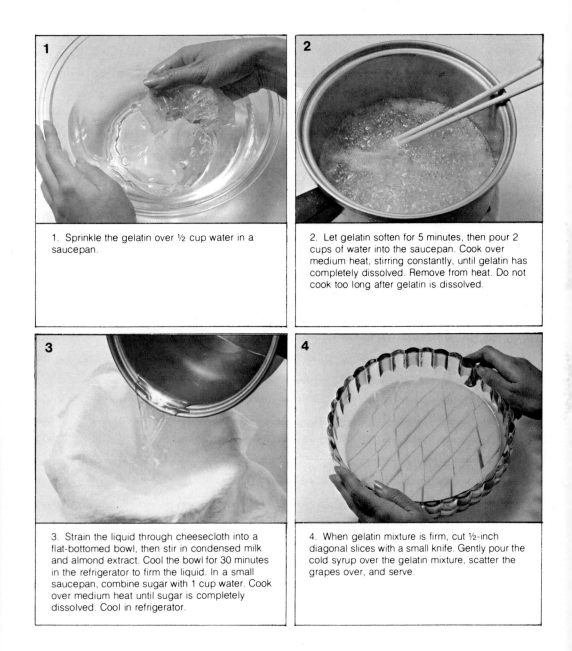

1. Sprinkle the gelatin over ½ cup water in a saucepan.

2. Let gelatin soften for 5 minutes, then pour 2 cups of water into the saucepan. Cook over medium heat, stirring constantly, until gelatin has completely dissolved. Remove from heat. Do not cook too long after gelatin is dissolved.

3. Strain the liquid through cheesecloth into a flat-bottomed bowl, then stir in condensed milk and almond extract. Cool the bowl for 30 minutes in the refrigerator to firm the liquid. In a small saucepan, combine sugar with 1 cup water. Cook over medium heat until sugar is completely dissolved. Cool in refrigerator.

4. When gelatin mixture is firm, cut ½-inch diagonal slices with a small knife. Gently pour the cold syrup over the gelatin mixture, scatter the grapes over, and serve.

Steamed Egg Cake (8-inch square)

COOKING TIME: 40 minutes
CALORIES PER SERVING: 1.052 for whole cake
PROTEIN PER SERVING: 33.9 g for whole cake

1 CUP FLOUR
1 TEASPOON BAKING POWDER
4 EGGS
½ CUP SUGAR
1 TEASPOON VEGETABLE OIL TO GREASE
   CAKE PAN
1 TEASPOON CANDIED CHERRIES OR
   OTHER EQUIVALENT FRUIT

SUGGESTIONS: Mandarin oranges or raisins can be substituted for the candied cherries. This cake is made in the steamer rather than the oven. Make sure not to over-mix egg mixture and flour or cake will become sticky.

1. Sift together the flour and the baking powder. Heat water in the steamer over medium heat.

2. Using a wire whisk, beat the eggs well. Add sugar gradually and beat until light and fluffy.

3. Gradually pour over the sifted flour the egg mixture. Using a wooden spoon fold in flour until none shows.

4. Grease the bottom and sides of an 8-inch-square cake pan. Greasing the pan makes it easier to remove the cake.

5. Sprinkle finely shredded candied cherries evenly over the bottom of the cake pan. Gently pour the cake mixture into the cake pan. Smooth the surface with wooden spoon.

6. The water for the steamer should be boiling by now. Place wax paper on bottom of the steamer rack (to make steaming gentler), and place the cake pan on top of the wax paper. Steam over high heat for 20 minutes. Do not remove the cover while steaming.

7. When cake is cooked, remove from the pan and let it cool. Cut the cake into 2-by-3-inch diamond-shaped pieces and serve.

5

7

Deep-fried Sesame Seed Biscuit (40 biscuits)

COOKING TIME: 30 minutes
CALORIES PER SERVING: 38 per biscuit
PROTEIN PER SERVING: 0.6 g per biscuit

2 CUPS FLOUR
½ CUP SUGAR
1 TABLESPOON ROASTED BLACK
   SESAME SEEDS
1 TABLESPOON LARD
1 EGG, BEATEN
VEGETABLE OIL FOR DEEP-FRYING

NOTE: Roast the sesame seeds in an ungreased, heavy skillet over medium heat until a few seeds start to jump. Do not let seeds burn. When you store, put them in container with tight cover.

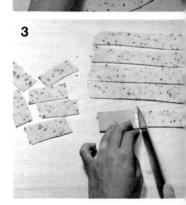

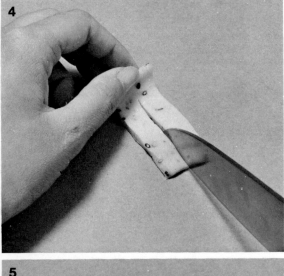

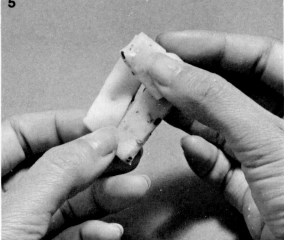

1. Sift the flour into a mixing bowl. Add sugar, roasted sesame seeds, lard, beaten egg, and a little water. Mix well with wooden spoon and transfer to lightly floured board. Knead well until dough becomes smooth, firm, and silky.

2. Using a lightly floured rolling pin, evenly roll the dough to a thickness of ¼-inch.

3. Cut the dough sheet into 1-by-2-inch rectangular pieces. Knead scraps again, reroll, and make more pieces.

4. Make a ¼-inch slit lengthwise in the center of every rectangular piece.

5. Fold one end through slit.

6. Pull both ends gently (see pictures 4, 5, and 6).

7. Heat oil in a wok to 350° and deep-fry the biscuits. When biscuits turn golden brown, remove from the oil and drain on paper towels. Cool before storing.

Mandarin Orange Float

COOKING TIME: 20 minutes
CALORIES PER SERVING: 476
PROTEIN PER SERVING: 4.9 g

½ CUP GLUTINOUS RICE FLOUR (SWEET
  RICE FLOUR)
11 OUNCES UNDRAINED MANDARIN
  ORANGES
¾ CUP SUGAR
2 TABLESPOONS CORNSTARCH

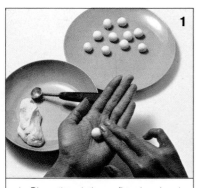

1. Place the glutinous flour in a bowl. Add ¼ cup water and knead well until dough becomes smooth and silky. Scoop out the dough with melon scooper or teaspoon and using palm of hand, make small balls, about ¾-inch in diameter.

2. Drop the balls in boiling water and cook until they rise to the surface of water. Drain, cool in cold water, and drain again.

3. Drain the mandarin oranges and reserve the juice. Add enough water to reserved juice to make 4 cups of liquid. Add the sugar to the liquid and bring to the boil over medium heat. When liquid begins to boil, mix cornstarch with 2 tablespoons water and add to the liquid. Heat until liquid clears and thickens. Add mandarin oranges and glutinous flour balls and remove from heat. Serve hot or chilled.

A Note on
Chinese Ingredients and Techniques

ABALONE

Abalone is a mollusk found in the Pacific Ocean especially near the coastlines of Mexico and Japan. The Chinese use it in their banquet dishes. The meat is attached to the shell. If used fresh after harvest, it has a smooth texture, but most abalone is canned. Since in canning the abalone has been cooked and seasoned, very little additional cooking is necessary. In fact, if overcooked, abalone will be leathery and inedible. If dried abalone is used, it has to be soaked in warm water for several hours and then cooked over low heat for several hours, before it can be used.

AGAR-AGAR

This is dried seaweed found in the Indian Ocean near India and in the Pacific Ocean near Japan. It is processed, dried, and packaged either in long noodlelike translucent strips thicker than cellophane noodles, or in squares about 1 inch in diameter and about 12 inches long. The strip type, if soaked in *cold* water, can be used in salads; the block type, when dissolved in hot water, can be used in place of gelatin.

BAMBOO SHOOTS

As its name implies, they are the tender shoots of the bamboo plant, grown in subtropical or tropical climates. The harvest season is short and in a few days the exposed shoots become woody and inedible. Fortunately, there are different bamboo plants that can be harvested during each season. The bamboo shoots used in the United States are mostly canned. Once the can is opened, any unused part remaining should be soaked in cold water and placed in the refrigerator. By changing the water, the shoots can be kept for several weeks.

BEAN CURD

A white custardlike square about 3 × 3 × 1 inches made from boiled soybean milk with a coagulate added. It comes as soft bean curd, often known as the Japanese bean curd, and the firm bean curd, known as Chinese bean curd. It has a very high vegetable protein content and is very nutritious. The soft bean curd is preferred for salads or soups, but the firmer kind is preferred for dishes with fish, meat, poultry, and/or vegetables. *Puffed bean curd* is 1 × 1 × 1 inch in size. It is made from firm bean curd, deep fried until the outside is golden brown and the inside is still soft and white. It is commercially made and comes in packages of several ounces or more. When using, soak in warm water with ½ teaspoon baking soda for 10 minutes, then rinse several times with cold water. Drain and add to meats, fish, or poultry. The bean curd will absorb the flavor of the accompanying ingredients in the dishes.

BEAN SPROUTS

There are two kinds of bean sprouts: those that are sprouts of soy beans and those that are sprouts of mung beans. The soy bean sprouts have two large yellow petals and much longer roots. Those that are sprouts of mung beans are sweeter, more tender, and crunchier. They are used in salads and with dishes such as Chop Suey, Chow Mein, and Fried Rice.

BEAN PASTE (Bean Sauce)

In Chinese cuisine, bean paste is also known as Bean Sauce. It is made from soy beans, salt, flour, and spices. It may also be known as brown sauce, yellow bean sauce, miso, and other names depending on the different spices added.

BOK CHOY (Chinese Cabbage)

This is a species of the swiss chard family. Many supermarkets now sell Bok Choy. It can be eaten raw in salads or can be cooked as a leafy vegetable. It keeps fresh in the vegetable compartment in the refrigerator for several days.

CELLOPHANE NOODLES

Cellophane noodles are so named because of their transparent appearance. They are made from mung bean flour. Mung beans are green in color and pealike in shape and size. Their starch content is lower than that of wheat, yet higher in vitamins. Cellophane noodles are sold in 2-ounce, 4-ounce, and half-pound packages. When soaked in warm water they swell up in size and become pliable; always drain before using. They are available in Oriental grocery stores and store indefinitely.

CHINESE CHIVES

This small flat green vegetable resembles American chives. These are stronger in flavor and can be used as a garnish or as a vegetable.

CHINESE CELERY CABBAGES

There are two species of celery cabbages on the market: those that are long, with green leaves are called Chinese Celery Cabbage; those that are short and fat, with white leaves are called Napa Cabbage because they are grown in Napa, California. This later species is more tender and juicy and is excellent in salads. Both kinds, if stir-fried the Chinese way, are excellent vegetables.

CHINESE MUSHROOMS

When the recipes in this book list Chinese mushrooms, it is a reference to certain kinds of black winter mushrooms, rich in flavor and thick and meaty in texture, that are often used in Chinese cooking. They are very expensive, but usually only a small amount is required in any dish. The dried mushrooms must be soaked in warm water for fifteen minutes, then drained. The mushrooms can be cut into various forms and sizes, depending upon their combination with the other ingredients.

CHINESE TURNIP

The best way to describe a Chinese turnip is to say that it resembles in color, shape, and texture the white icicle radish found in supermarkets during the spring. The only difference is that the Chinese turnip is much larger in size. The latter are about three inches in diameter and ten to fifteen inches long. They are excellent as salads or made into soup with meat or chicken stock; they are also good as vegetables, served with meat, fish, or poultry.

DRIED RED HOT PEPPER

Dried red hot peppers and dried chili peppers are the same thing. They are available in all markets, either whole or in flakes. Since these peppers are very strong, care should be used not to use too much pepper.

DRIED SHRIMPS

The best dried shrimps without shells are produced in New Orleans, Louisiana. They are imported to the Orient. To get good results, soak the shrimps in a little dry sherry for twenty minutes before using. The flavor of the shrimps will then be absorbed easier by the vegetables with which they are cooked.

DRIED RICE NOODLES

Rice noodles differ from wheat or cellophane noodles in that they are made from rice flour. They are usually sold in dried form made in China. Except when they are to be deep-fried, they should be pre-soaked for about fifteen minutes in warm water and then drained before using. It is best to stir-fry rice noodles with pork and other vegetables and serve like lo mein noodles as a snack or as a substitute for a rice dish in a meal.

GINGEROOT, FRESH

Gingeroot is a knobby, irregular-shaped rhizome of the ginger plant. It grows well in subtropical climates. A few slices added to the cooking oil for fish, meat, or poultry dishes enhance greatly their flavor.

A few slices will go a long way. Dried ginger or ginger powder cannot substitute for the fresh ginger. To store the root for a long period, peel the outer skin and keep the piece in a wide-mouthed jar, covered with dry sherry. Cover and store in the refrigerator; the ginger will be fresh for a long time. *Ginger juice* is squeezed from fresh gingeroot with a garlic press. It is used for special recipes which designate the use of ginger in liquid.

GLUTINOUS RICE

Glutinous rice is sometimes called sweet, or sticky, rice. It is a short-grained rice, opaque in color. It is mostly used for stuffing although often it is also used for desserts. Since the glutinous rice is short grain, less water should be used when cooking.

HOT PEPPER OIL

Hot pepper oil is made with dried chili peppers and vegetable oil. Most hot oil is commercially made but you can try to make it at home. Soak the dried hot pepper in oil for one hour, then cook for thirty minutes on top of the stove, over very low heat. Let the pepper soak in oil for twenty-four hours, then strain the pepper and store the dark red oil in a bottle for later use.

JELLYFISH

What comes to the market is either the round, thin skin of the jellyfish or the body and tenacles. Both parts are dried and heavily marinated in coarse salt for a couple of weeks. They are dried in the sun and then packed for shipping. When bought in the market, jellyfish should be washed thoroughly in cold water, then shredded or cut into ½- × 2-inch pieces and again soaked in cold water and left in the refrigerator. The bland but crisp texture is highlighted in salads or by adding the jellyfish to a sauce mixture of sesame seed oil, soy sauce, and sugar.

LO MEIN NOODLES

These are fine noodles made with eggs, flour, and water and they are chiefly used in making the dish Lo Mein. They can be bought in Oriental stores by the pound. Leave them in a plastic bag and store in the refrigerator for a week. They can also be stored frozen for a month.

CHINESE MUSTARD

Chinese mustard is a paste used as a table condiment in Chinese restaurants. It is made by blending English mustard powder with a little water. It is rather strong and should be used sparingly.

QUAIL EGGS

These are the eggs of a small bird, the quail, which are often used as a delicacy at Chinese banquets. The eggs must first be hard-boiled, then shelled before they are used. They come in cans in liquid and can be bought in Oriental markets.

RICE VINEGAR

The vinegar the Chinese use is made mainly from rice. The color of this vinegar is dark brown and the consistency is rather thick.

SAKE

Sake is a wine made from rice used mostly in Japan as a beverage and for cooking purposes. In China Shao-shing wine, which is also made from rice, is used as a beverage and for cooking. Both these wines should be warmed before drinking. If neither Sake nor Shao-shing is available, dry sherry is an acceptable substitute.

SCALLIONS

Scallions, sometimes called spring onions or green onions, are used extensively in Chinese cooking. If they are to be minced fine and mixed with other ingredients, only the green parts should be used. But when a strong onion taste is required both the white and the green parts should be used.

SESAME SEEDS — BLACK AND WHITE

Sesame seeds are the seeds of an Asian herb plant. They are grown both in Asia and in the United States. The white sesame seeds are more popular, but the black seeds have a stronger flavor. They can be ground and made into paste, and be used interchangeably with peanut butter.

SESAME SEED OIL

The difference between the Oriental sesame seed oil and that from the Near East is that the Oriental oil is made from roasted sesame seeds. The color is darker and the flavor stronger.

SHAO MEI WRAPPERS

Shao mei wrappers are made from a dough consisting of egg, flour, and water. It is rolled out into a very thin sheet and it is cut into individual pieces with a cutter of about three inches in diameter. The wrappers are available in Chinese grocery stores and can be kept in the refrigerator for a few days or in the freezer for several weeks.

SNOW PEAS

Snow Peas are a type of garden pea cultivated in the Orient especially for its edible pod. They are harvested when the pea pods are about three inches in length and one-half inch in width. They are a bright green in color and are an addition to many Chinese dishes. When using, they should be stringed and added in the last couple of minutes to prevent the pods from overcooking and becoming limp; an important feature of these pods is their crunchiness.

SOY SAUCE

Chinese soy sauce is a brown, salted liquid made from soy beans. Although in the past Chinese made their own soy sauce, it is a complicated job. The dried soy beans must be soaked, boiled, and then fermented. They are resteamed, and salt and spices are added, then left in crocks for weeks for more fermentation. At the end of the process the mixture is resteamed. All the residue is removed and the soy sauce is ready for use. There are "light" soy sauces and "dark" soy sauces. The difference is not so much in the color since they are both brown, bur rather in the thickness of the liquid. The light soy sauce is used more as a table condiment, while a combination of the light and dark soy sauces is used in cooking.

STAR ANISE

Star anise is a dry, brown seed cluster in the shape of an eight-pointed star. It is a spice of licorice-flavor often used by Chinese in cooking poultry and meat. Like all spices it should be used sparingly. The flavor is what is desirable, so discard the star anise before serving the dish.

SWEET RED BEAN

Red bean is a species of bean whose outer skin is red. Usually we find dried red beans in the market. Soak in warm water for an hour, then drain and add enough water in a sauce pan to generously cover the beans. Cook on top of the stove over low heat and simmer for about forty minutes, or until the beans are very soft. Add sugar to taste.

SZECHUAN PEPPERCORN

This is a highly aromatic, reddish-brown pepper-corn sold in the Chinese market. It is the product of the Szechuan Province of China. Its unique quality is that while it is mildly hot and scented, the spicy hotness flashes away after a while. If stored in covered bottles, it will last for years without losing its flavor.

SZECHUAN PRESERVED KOHLRABI

A very hot pickle made by preserving kohlrabi in Szechuan peppercorn, chili pepper, and coarse salt. The fresh kohlrabi must first be wilted for a day and packed in a large crock mixed with Szechuan Peppercorn, chili, and salt. The top of the crock is then sealed with water. (Note: to waterseal pour water into a canal-like ring on top of the crock and cover with an inverted bowl; this makes it airtight.)

TARO

This is a root of a tropical plant, similar to a potato but larger in size and darker in color. It is sold in Oriental markets. The outer skin must be peeled as with potato and then used in different ways as the recipe calls for. The canned version is a good substitute.

TREE EARS

This is a small dried black fungus irregular in shape. It is called a tree ear because it grows on the exposed roots of trees in Szechuan Province. When dried it resembles dried tea, but if soaked it will swell to four times its size. It is therefore important not to soak too many tree ears at one time.

THOUSAND-YEAR-OLD EGG

Thousand-year-old eggs are made from fresh duck eggs coated for about one-quarter inch with a mixture of lime, salt, grain husks, and mud. They are kept in a dark place for about six weeks. The process of capillary action cooks and turns the white of the eggs to amber color and the yolk to green; it is cheese-like in texture. After this period, the preserved eggs can be cracked, mud and shell removed, and eaten with ginger shreds and soy sauce as appetizer.

WONTON WRAPPER

These are made from a dough mixture of egg, flour, and water with a sprinkling of salt. After the dough is rolled out, it is cut into 3 × 3 inch-squares, stacked, then wrapped for future use. They will be good for a few days in the refrigerator and several weeks in the freezer.

TEA

Tea is the national beverage of China. Although there are over two hundred brand names of tea used in China, there are only three basic types of tea. The Green or unfermented tea, the Oolung or semifermented tea, and the Black tea or fully fermented tea. Tea must be fresh, so buy it in small quantities and keep in airtight canisters. Use about half a teaspoon per cup of tea and add a little boiling water, letting it steep for five to seven minutes. Fill the cup or pot with hot water before pouring.

THE FOLLOWING ARE THE IMPORTANT WAYS OF COOKING THE CHINESE WAY.

STIR-FRYING

As the name implies this technique involves stirring and frying the food at the same time. Use a little oil in the frying pan or wok. Toss the food continuously over very high heat for a short time. In these very few minutes add whatever ingredients to the pan as specified in the recipe. Mix thoroughly before finishing the cooking. This type of cooking should be done at the last minute and the food be served immediately.

WET-STEAMING

The steamer comes in two or more sections. The upper sections have their bottoms perforated; the lowest section is used as a large pan to hold water. By boiling the water in the lower section, the steam rises into the upper sections. The food is usually placed in the upper sections with or without plates. With the hot steam coming through the holes, the food is cooked.

DEEP-FRYING

Heat one or more cups oil in a quart-sized saucepan to 375 degrees and drop a few pieces of the food gently into the oil. When the pieces are golden brown, lift out and drain on a paper towel. Fried food should be served immediately.

SHALLOW-FRYING

Pour enough oil to cover the bottom of the frying pan. Spread the food evenly in the pan and let it fry over medium heat for a few minutes, or until the food is golden brown. Then turn over and repeat the process. If necessary, drain the food on paper towels.

RED-COOKING

This technique is very much like stewing. It requires a very heavy pot with a tight-fitting lid. The food and ingredients are first evenly browned, then the required amount of water is added. The food is cooked first over medium, then over low heat for a given length of time. There is a distinct advantage to this technique, as food can be prepared a day or two ahead and re-heated on top of the stove.

CLEAR SIMMERING

This is an important method of making soup. Only water is used with the food to be cooked. After a long period of simmering over low heat, add the ingredients and then cook over low heat for another short period of time. It is best to cook a day ahead. After cooling, leave in the refrigerator; then the excess fat will congeal on top of the soup and can be discarded. This makes the soup grease free but retains the flavor of the meat and vegetables.

CUTTING IS A VERT IMPORTANT PART OF CHINESE COOKING. FOR THOUSANDS OF YEARS CHINESE COOKS USED TWIGS, WOOD, BAMBOO, AND EVEN LEAVES. THESE HAD TO BE COLLECTED, DRIED, AND STORED BEFORE THEY COULD BE USED. WHEN FOODS ARE CUT INTO SMALLER PIECES, THE COOKING IS FASTER, THUS LESS FUEL IS NEEDED. THE MAJOR WAYS OF CUTTING ARE AS FOLLOWS;

SLICING

There are two ways to slice — the straight slice and the slant slice. In straight slicing, the food is sliced into thin pieces when the cleaver or knife is at a ninety-degree angle to the food. The cuts are usually in the form of rounds, squares, and rectangulars. Slant slicing is different from straight slicing in that the cleaver or knife is at only forty-five-degree angle to the food. The result is that the slices are either oblong or larger rectangles.

SHREDDING

This method involves taking the slant-sliced food and again cutting it into shreds from one-fourth inch to one-eighth inch in width. The size depends upon the combination of the food used in any dish.

DICING

Food can be cut into large or small cubes. Using coarse or thin shreds cut perpendicular to them and cut into larger or smaller cubes.

OBLIQUE CUTTING

This way of cutting is to obtain more surface area for fibrous vegetables and coarser meat to absorb flavor in slow cooking. Start cutting slant pieces off any round or thick pieces of food, then roll a quarter of the diameter toward the cutter, and cut off another piece. Continue rolling and cutting until the whole piece is thus cut. Carrots and bamboo shoots are the best examples for this type of cutting.

Index